WEAPON

WINCHESTER LEVER-ACTION RIFLES

MARTIN PEGLER

OSPREY PUBLISHING
Bloomsbury Publishing Plc

Kemp House, Chawley Park, Oxford OX2 9PH, UK
29 Earlsfort Terrace, Dublin 2, Ireland
1385 Broadway, 5th Floor, New York, NY 10018, USA
Email: info@ospreypublishing.com
www.ospreypublishing.com

OSPREY is a trademark of Osprey Publishing Ltd

First published in Great Britain in 2015
Transferred to digital print in 2023

A CIP catalog record for this book is available from the British Library

Print ISBN: 978 1 4728 0657 4
PDF eBook ISBN: 978 1 4728 0658 1
ePub ISBN: 978 1 4728 0659 8

Index by Rob Munro
Battlescenes by Mark Stacey
Cutaway artwork by Alan Gilliland
Originated by PDQ Media, Bungay, UK
Typeset in Sabon and Univers
Printed in Great Britain by CPI (Group) UK Ltd, Croydon CR0 4YY

23 24 25 26 27   15 14 13 12 11 10 9 8

Osprey Publishing supports the Woodland Trust, the UK's leading woodland conservation charity.

www.ospreypublishing.com

The NRA Museums

Since 1935, the NRA Museum collection has become one of the world's finest museum collections dedicated to firearms. Now housed in three locations, the NRA Museums offer a glimpse into the firearms that built our nation, helped forge our freedom, and captured our imagination. The **National Firearms Museum**, located at the NRA Headquarters in Fairfax, Virginia, details and examines the nearly 700-year history of firearms with a special emphasis on firearms, freedom, and the American experience. The **National Sporting Arms Museum**, at the Bass Pro Shops in Springfield, Missouri, explores and exhibits the historical development of hunting arms in America from the earliest explorers to modern day, with a focus on hunting, conservation, and freedom. The **Frank Brownell Museum of the Southwest**, at the NRA Whittington Center in Raton, NM, is a jewel box museum with 200 guns that tells the history of the region from the earliest Native American inhabitants through early Spanish exploration, the Civil War, and the Old West. For more information on the NRA Museums and hours, visit **www.NRAmuseums.com.**

Acknowledgments

I would like to offer special thanks to my friends Laurie Landau, for access to her splendid Winchester collection, and Dr. Bob Maze, for spending so much time in photographing them. Also to Roy Jinks for allowing me to reproduce images from his seminal Smith and Wesson book, and to the National Rifle Association for access to their collection of firearms images. I am also greatly indebted to Lisa Traynor and Jonathan Ferguson, curators at the Royal Armouries/National Firearms Collection in Leeds, UK, for pictures of some of their extensive cartridge collection. I am also grateful for being able to use some of the fine work done in 2011 by Andrew L. Bresnan and Todd Koster in "The Henry Repeating Rifle," which is available online at www.44henryrifle.webs.com/civilwarusage.htm. Special thanks to Michael F. Carrick and Stefan Brinski, who were very helpful in supplying me with information and rare pictures of Winchesters used in French and Russian military service. Finally, thanks as always to my uncomplaining wife Katie for the endless cups of tea and accepting that I spend more time with my keyboard than with her. I have of course tried to ensure all of the facts in this book are accurate, but if there are any errors, the mistake is entirely mine.

Artist's note

Readers may care to note that the original paintings from which the battlescenes in this book were prepared are available for private sale. All reproduction copyright whatsoever is retained by the Publishers. All inquiries should be addressed to:

mark@mrstacey.plus.com

The Publishers regret that they can enter into no correspondence upon this matter.

Editor's note

In this book a mixture of metric and US customary measurements is used. For ease of comparison please use the following conversion table:

1 mile = 1.6km
1yd = 0.91m
1ft = 0.30m
1in = 2.54cm/25.4mm
1lb = 0.45kg

Cover images. Top: A Winchester Model 1873 (NRA Museums, NRAmuseums.com). Bottom: A youthful John Wayne in a studio portrait, carrying one of his favorite screen Winchesters, a Model 1892 (© Corbis).

Title-page image: Taken by N.A. Forsyth in the early 1900s, this portrait entitled "Bear Chief and His Hudson Bay Coat" depicts a Piegan Blackfoot as he stands, Model 1873 Winchester at his side, before his horse in a campsite, Browning, Montana. Interestingly, he carries a revolver in an improvised, but practical early version of a shoulder holster. (Photo by Transcendental Graphics/Getty Images)

CONTENTS

INTRODUCTION

From the very inception of the firearm, one of the holy grails for manufacturers was to overcome the constraints imposed by the available technology and create a firearm that had the ability to fire repeatedly. The introduction of the perfected flintlock in the early 18th century did much to improve the reliability and efficient functioning of firearms, but loading and shooting were still tediously slow and much affected by wind and weather, which could blow priming powder from pans or soak the propellant. Gunmakers dreamed of being able to produce guns, both handguns and long-arms, that were able to be charged once and then repeatedly fired. Despite advances in manufacturing techniques, technological progress in the firearms industry was hampered by the only available propellant: gunpowder, a horrible chemical concoction incorporating all of the traits that were most undesirable in a propellant. It was dangerously volatile, usually when it wasn't required to be, but was also hygroscopic (or water absorbing), making it extremely non-volatile, usually at the most inopportune moments. Furthermore, its slow burn rate resulted in relatively low velocities, and it produced a vast cloud of white smoke on firing. Even worse, it left behind a thick, sooty residue that choked gun barrels and touch holes and was highly corrosive if left uncleaned for more than a few hours. But it was all that was available, so for 500 years all firearms makers were forced to work within its confines.

In the late 17th and early 18th centuries a few gunmakers very nearly achieved the impossible by producing revolving-cylinder pistols that relied on flintlock mechanisms. They were large, temperamental, expensive, and generally regarded as no more than novelties, but attempting to do the same with a long-arm was even more problematic. Using the revolving-cylinder system created too much weight and unacceptable loss of propellant gas from the gap between the cylinder and breech. Clearly, some form of breech-loading method was necessary, but this was a problem gunmakers had been wrestling with, mostly without success, for

200 years. Aside from the purely mechanical problems, much of the difficulty lay in the primitive cartridges in use. While paper-wrapped combustible ammunition worked tolerably well in a musket that was loaded and fired fairly quickly afterward, when used in a repeating arm, if the charge was left for any length of time, its hygroscopic properties rendered it useless, requiring the bullet to be removed and the chambers laboriously cleaned out. Even when fired, the gun would need cleaning at frequent intervals to prevent touch holes being blocked, and loading was a tedious process.

As technology advanced and firearms design improved through the early 19th century, many of these problems were gradually overcome. Developed in the mid-1820s, percussion ignition did away with the need for separate powder priming, and revolving cylinder handguns became both reliable and commonplace in the first part of the 19th century. Several types of quite efficient breech-loading rifles appeared by the 1820s, but it was a small invention by a Frenchman, Louis Nicolas Flobert (1819–94), that would revolutionize firearms design forever. His idea was quite simple. For gallery and target shooting he placed a small spherical lead bullet straight onto a percussion cap, so no propellant powder was required. It worked brilliantly, but of course was of use only for very short ranges, which was entirely its purpose. The self-contained metallic

This classic Western image is actually of a Frenchman, Antoine Amédée de Vallombrosa, the Marquis de Mores. He was a titled rancher in the Dakota badlands who gained a reputation as a hot-headed gunslinger and duelist and was arrested several times for murder. He has a Model 1876 rifle resting on his shoulder. (State History Society of North Dakota)

Winchester's .30-30, arguably the most significant commercial cartridge ever introduced. It is still the most widely used caliber for hunting in the United States. (Author)

cartridge finally made it possible to design efficient systems that were able to accept multiple charges and feed them (more or less) reliably through the mechanical action of a long-arm.

One of the first rifles to achieve this was the rimfire Spencer, adopted in considerable numbers during the American Civil War (1861–65), and it was during this incredibly fertile period that another rimfire rifle, the Henry, made a tentative appearance on the battlefield. In fact, this new rifle owed its antecedence to a series of developments that were far more complex than simply the creation of the metallic cartridge, harking back to 1848 when a primitive, but workable repeating rifle called the Volition was produced in a prototype form. It took a dozen years for the design to be honed to the point where the mechanism was reliable enough to be introduced to the commercial marketplace. Even then it was limited by the lack of suitable ammunition, for only relatively low-powered rimfire cartridges were readily available. Nevertheless, the ability for a man to have a rifle that could be loaded with 16 cartridges and fired as fast as the action could be cycled was extraordinary and potent, and demand for these repeating rifles continued to grow after the end of the Civil War. Alas, the trouble as always was that few engineers were businessmen, and many companies set up to manufacture improved firearms designs had collapsed within a year or two.

The Henry Company was no exception and would have sunk without trace had not an entrepreneur and shirt manufacturer named Oliver Winchester become the major shareholder of the old company. In taking control he also acquired the considerable engineering abilities of Benjamin Tyler Henry. Winchester was no engineer, but he was an astute businessman who understood the need to employ people who could ensure the product was reliable and viable. In this he was providentially helped through the early 1870s by ammunition improvements that saw the demise of the old rimfire cartridges and the introduction of new and more powerful centerfire types. This advance enabled the company to expand its range of models and calibers, but it ironically also exacerbated the inherent mechanical weaknesses in the design of the rifles. Winchester was always prepared to employ the best and he took on the brilliant John Moses Browning to try to overcome the shortcomings of the lever-action used in the Winchesters, which, up to a point, he was able to do. Although Winchester died in 1880, his company, Winchester Repeating Arms, continued to go from strength to strength.

DEVELOPMENT
"The ability to shoot repeatedly"

FORERUNNERS

The Volition Repeating Rifle

Several inventors and gunmakers noted Flobert's ingenious idea with interest and one, an obsessive New York City amateur engineer by the name of Walter Hunt (1796–1859), decided to take the Frenchman's idea a stage further. In 1848 Hunt patented a bullet/cartridge called the Rocket Ball, which used a Minié-type bullet, conical with a deep hollow base, packed with gunpowder, and with a percussion cap fitted into the base. Hunt was not primarily a firearms designer (he patented the safety pin, which he thought of little use and sold the patent for $400, about $10,000/£6,400 in today's money). What he produced was an awkwardly balanced but tolerably efficient breech-loading repeating rifle, known as the Volition, that chambered his new ammunition in a tubular magazine. Hunt used a novel system for loading and cocking the gun, with a forward trigger ring that lowered a carrier inside the receiver, permitting a bullet to be fed onto it from the under-barrel magazine. Pulling on a second ring raised the carrier, chambered the bullet and cocked the action. It was cumbersome and fairly slow to use, with bullets often jamming as they were extracted, but it did have the rare ability to shoot as fast as the lever action could be cycled, assuming the ammunition worked, which it frequently didn't. It was not entirely surprising that these newly created Volition rifles did not sell well; at this point, his idea might simply have vanished from history but for the fact that the patent rights had been assigned to Hunt's backer, a businessman named George Arrowsmith who, wanting to cover his losses, had promptly sold them to a railroad tycoon, Courtlandt Palmer (1800–74), for the then considerable sum of $100,000 ($3.1 million/£1.9 million today).

The Jennings Rifle

Palmer knew another, rather more talented, gun designer called Lewis Jennings who was intrigued by the Hunt design; Jennings realized very quickly that the low power of the Rocket Ball was the most serious shortcoming in promoting the other advantages of the new repeating long-arm, for the feeble energy it produced was roughly half that of a modern .22 Long Rifle cartridge. It was useful perhaps for dispatching mice, but that was about all it was capable of. So Richard S. Lawrence (1817–72), an innovative gunmaker and half of the successful Robbins and Lawrence gunmaking concern, commenced to improve the rifle. By the end of 1849, Lawrence had redesigned and patented his own version of the gun. Its first incarnation was that of a conventional single-shot, breech-loading design using a standard percussion nipple, but the second and third patterns Jennings made were far more advanced.

He fitted a 20-shot tubular magazine underneath the barrel and although still retaining the percussion ignition, he modified it to use an automatic-feed primer strip of "pill" pattern not unlike today's modern toy cap guns. It still used the distinctive ring lever-action to load and cock the mechanism, which operated a horizontally sliding breech-block that extracted the cartridge then chambered it. Unlike Hunt's design, which relied on a clumsy two-ring operating system, Jennings' weapon was able to combine the extraction and loading into one fluid motion utilizing a single ring, or lever. The entire rifle weighed 9lb and had a 34in barrel. More crucially, Jennings abandoned the Rocket Ball, and came up with his own .54-caliber self-contained cartridge, a far more potent although still relatively underpowered bullet compared to that used in a muzzle-loading rifle.

The story now becomes a little convoluted, for neither Jennings nor Palmer had the ability to fund the manufacture of the rifles in quantity, and they were forced to seek help from a company prepared to make a relatively mechanically complex rifle. There was no shortage of gunmakers – at the time there were 300 registered companies producing firearms in Vermont alone – but the majority were manufacturing simple muzzle-loaders, and the Jennings rifle was anything but simple. It required a manufacturer with considerable expertise and a workforce with the relevant skills. They approached an established gunmaking firm in Windsor, Vermont, named Robbins, Kendall, & Lawrence, who had achieved some prominence in 1844 when in the face of much opposition from other contractors, they bid for and won a contract for 10,000 Government rifles, despite having no prior mass-production experience. They developed new methods of production and assembly using machine tools that resulted in all parts being interchangeable, combining rapid assembly with great precision. When they couldn't obtain the machinery

they wanted, they designed and built it themselves. Indeed, so advanced were their methods that many of their machines were copied, and a few are still in use today. They were the ideal partners for Jennings and Palmer, and an order for 5,000 was placed by Courtlandt Palmer. Sadly, the rifle proved to be a commercial failure, for several reasons. It was an unattractive design that did not appeal to buyers, and to load and fire one required the shooter to go through a complex series of movements, which were not instinctive. Nevertheless, there were converts. A Jennings was tested by the staff of *American International Magazine*, who reported its operation in some detail in their issue of January 1, 1852:

The percussion mechanism and later-type loading lever can clearly be seen on this Jennings. Because of the many problems associated with the original design some Jennings, such as this one, were converted to simple muzzle-loaders. (NRA Museums, NRAmuseums.com)

> Fill the magazine, on the top of the breech, with percussion pills or primings, and the tube, under the barrel, with the hollow cartridges containing gunpowder. Of these cartridges the tube will hold twenty-four. Place the forefinger in the ring which forms the end of the lever, e, and the thumb on the hammer, elevating the muzzle sufficiently to let the cartridge nearest the breech slip, by its gravity, into the carrier d; swing the lever forward, and raise the hammer which moves the breech-pin back, and the carrier up, placing the cartridge into the barrel, by which motion a percussion priming is taken from the magazine by means of the priming-rack, revolving the pinion which forms the bottom of the magazine, and it also throws up the toggle, behind the breech-pin, thus placing the piece in the condition to be discharged by a simple upward pressure of the finger in the ring. After the discharge release the pressure and repeat the process.

Despite the Jennings rifle's complexity, the magazine rather liked it – or at least the lever-action concept – and this attitude was echoed in later tests by other publications. But the reality was that the complex mechanism required meticulous care and suffered from a series of minor mechanical failures; despite using an uprated bullet, the Jennings self-contained design simply could not hold sufficient charge to enable it to be a practical hunting

9

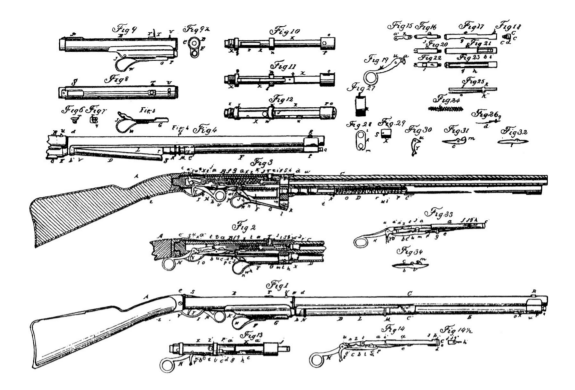

The 1849 patent for the original Jennings design. The close proximity of the cartridges in the magazine, which would cause problems later on, and the extremely complex toggle mechanism can clearly be seen. (Author)

or self-defense rifle. It was in production from 1850 to 1852; only about 1,000 were made. While the rifle itself was not a success, the concept had begun to establish itself as something that was attainable and potentially practical, if only the problems could be ironed out. Of particular interest to this story was the fact that the foreman at the Windsor factory during this period was an engineer named Benjamin Tyler Henry.

The Volcanic Rifle

The demise of the Jennings rifle did not result in the abandonment of the repeating-rifle concept, however. In 1850 Palmer had hired another engineer, Horace Smith (1808–93), to supervise the production and improve on the action of the Jennings rifle, but even his intervention was not enough to save the design. Nevertheless, Smith's involvement was crucial to the future of the concept, for he simplified the mechanism, enabling the rifle to be loaded and cocked by just using a single trigger ring. Smith had a long pedigree of working on complex firearms and the Jennings fueled his idea for producing a repeating revolver based on the design. It is also probable that while working for Robbins and Lawrence, he first met Daniel B. Wesson (1825–1906). Daniel had an established gunmaking business with his brother Edwin (1811–49) in Massachusetts, and Daniel Wesson and Horace Smith struck an immediate friendship that resulted in a partnership in 1852. Both men recognized the potential of the Jennings design, but there were some major hurdles to overcome if it was to become commercially viable. Refining the mechanism was really just a matter of time and experiment and it was not a difficult process.

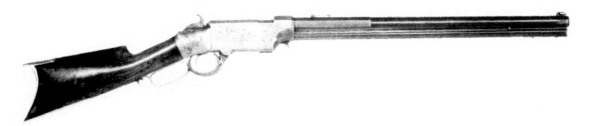

Indeed, Smith had already worked out a means by which the whole operation could be simplified into one fluid movement. More difficulty lay in finding some form of ammunition that was powerful enough to be practical in a long-arm, but it was almost impossible to find a self-contained cartridge that would work. After a solid year of work, the company was dangerously close to failure and they turned again to a familiar name, Courtlandt Palmer. Fortunately, he had faith in the concept and refinanced the project, enabling the team to continue work on the rifles. In 1852 they produced a very workmanlike and modern-looking .50-caliber rifle and it is from this that all subsequent later Winchester models were derived, although that was still a considerable time away.

The Volcanic rifle used an improved mechanism with tubular magazine that was loaded from the front. The basic mechanical function relied on a toggle link with a vertically sliding cartridge carrier, which acted in the same manner as the platform in a box magazine, the magazine having an internal spring. The spring had to be manually pushed forward when loading; when released it exerted pressure on the nose of the foremost cartridge, forcing it and any others in the magazine rearward and exerting a constant pressure on them to ensure they were always correctly positioned for loading. Should the spring fail then the cartridge would slide uselessly to and fro in the magazine tube, making reloading impossible unless the rifle was held vertically. The breech-bolt slid longitudinally within the receiver and was locked and unlocked by the toggle link attached to an under-lever. The carrier in the closed position lay flat behind the magazine tube; when the under-lever was pushed forward the toggle link folded up and pulled the bolt to the rear, which in turn pushed the hammer rearward into the full-cock position. When the shooter pulled the lever rearward it straightened the toggle and pushed the bolt forward, which then pushed the cartridge off the carrier platform and into the chamber. The last action of closing the lever enabled the now empty carrier to be pulled down where the magazine spring pushed another cartridge onto it in readiness.

Although as a verbal explanation it appears complex, mechanically this was actually a relatively simple system. The difficulty was in ensuring it functioned reliably, and in this Smith and Wesson were hampered by the failure of the available metallic cartridges to work properly. In desperation, they turned to the original Rocket Ball concept, and patented a bullet that contained a powder charge and held in a metal cup, a percussion cap and cork base washer. Patented in January 1856, the bullet proved considerably more powerful and reliable than the Flobert pattern, but it was still underpowered for a rifle. Nevertheless, it was the best solution then

An extremely rare example of the .50-caliber Smith and Wesson lever-action rifle, dated *c*.1852. It chambered the improved Wesson cartridge, which unlike the primitive Volcanic, used a copper cartridge case. At a quick glance it could easily be mistaken for a Henry, although it pre-dates the first model by eight years. (Roy Jinks)

Volcanic Repeating Fire-Arms.

Rifles and Pistols carrying from 7 to 30 Balls. Thirty Balls can be loaded and fired in less than one minute.

REPEATING FIRE-ARMS,
AND PATENT LOADED BALL.

Push the spring up in the tube by the knob A, till the top or cap B can be turned to the left, then put the number of cartridges you wish to use in the tube, replace the cap B, when the spring will follow the cartridge down; raise the hammer C, and swing the lever D clear forward, which will elevate the carrier E with a cartridge; pull the lever D clear back, which forces the cartridge into the barrel and braces the breech-pin F, when the arm is in condition for discharge. The balls should never be carried in any position to get the grease wiped off. The arm will never miss fire if these directions are observed.

JOSEPH MERWIN,
267 BROADWAY, NEW YORK, Sole Agent.

The rapidity of execution of this Arm places it beyond all competition. The thirty-shooter can be loaded and fired in less than one minute—a quickness and force of execution which is as much superior to the best revolvers as they are to the old muzzle-loading single shooters.

The Ammunition is water-proof, hence it can be used in any weather, or loaded and hung up for months, or laid under water, and then fired with certainty.

Its safety from accidental discharge is a great consideration in its favor; for, while the magazine (a tube running the whole length of the barrel) may be filled with balls, and thus the gun, in fact, be loaded from breech to muzzle, it is yet impossible, from any carelessness in handling, to discharge it. *Its construction* is simple and its workmanship most perfect, hence it is not easily got out of repair.

Its proportions are light, elegant, and compact, and the barrels are all rifled with great exactness. It requires no cap nor priming, no bullet-mould nor powder-flask. The powder and cap is contained in a loaded "minnie" ball of the best form and proportions, and is as sure as the best percussion caps.

It shoots with accuracy and greater force than any other arm can with double the powder used in this. Directions for use accompany each arm. Balls are packed in tin cases, 200 each.

After this date, the price will be as follows, viz. :

No. 1,	4-inch Pocket Pistol,	$12 00,	Plated and Engraved,	$13 50,	Carrying	6 Balls.
No. 1,	6 " for Target Practice,	13 50,	" " "	15 00,	"	10 "
No. 2,	6 " Navy Pistol,	18 00,	" " "	20 00,	"	8 "
No. 2,	8 " " "	18 00,	" " "	20 60,	"	10 "
No. 2,	16 " Carbine,	30 00,	" " "	33 00,	"	20 "
No. 2,	20 " "	35 00,	" " "	38 00,	"	25 "
No. 2,	24 " "	40 00,	" " "	43 00,	"	30 "

AMMUNITION.

No. 1 Balls, 130 to the Pound, $10 per Thousand. No. 2 Balls, 66 to the Pound, $12 per Thousand.

No. 1 Arms require No. 1 Balls. No. 2 Arms require No. 2 Balls.)

A liberal discount to the trade. Your orders are respectfully solicited.

(TURN OVER.)

An advertisement for the Volcanic Repeating Firearms Company. It shows the uncomplicated but weak toggle mechanism quite clearly, as well as the patented "loaded ball" ammunition contained in the magazine. It remained fundamentally unchanged until John Browning began work to strengthen the action. (Author)

available. Rapid firing created clouds of smoke and sparks from the muzzle, resembling a small volcano erupting, and inevitably this resulted in the sobriquet "Volcanic." The gun worked tolerably well, although misfires still caused problems. In order to facilitate sales, Smith and Wesson formed the Volcanic Repeating Arms Company in June 1855; in an early example of astute marketing, the new guns were offered to dozens of popular magazines for testing. Generally, they were well received. *Frank Leslie's Illustrated Newspaper*, one of the largest-selling magazines of its

day, positively enthused about the rifle, bordering on the ecstatic about the Volcanic cartridge, stating in its issue of October 9, 1858:

A .31-caliber Smith & Wesson Volcanic pocket pistol, illustrating the double-ring loading lever. (NRA Museums, NRAmuseums.com)

> It combines every quality requisite in such a weapon, with many advantages which no similar invention has yet succeeded in attaining. Thirty shots can be fired in less than one minute – a really marvellous rapidity in which it far outdoes the best revolving firearms yet produced. Its ammunition has the advantage of compactness, lightness and of being water-proof. The entire charge consists ... a bullet of the Minié pattern, in which both the charge and priming are contained, and of which sixty weigh only one pound. What an improvement on the heavy cartridge or powder flask that it has hither been necessary to carry! The balls may be soaked in water with perfect impunity, and can be kept any length of time in any climate without losing their explosive force.

However, both Smith and Wesson had considerably more experience working on pistols than long-arms and they knew that in reality their improved bullet design was only suitable for use in a pistol. Despite the time spent trying to perfect the rifles, Smith and Wesson continued to work on their pistol designs, and they miniaturized the lever-action. By February 1854 they had produced and patented two Volcanic pistols, one in .41 caliber and a smaller-framed variant in .31 caliber. The ammunition was still a major stumbling block, though, and both men knew that some form of reliable, self-contained metallic cartridge was needed to permit efficient functioning of the pistols. So, in August 1854 Smith and Wesson patented their own design of self-contained metallic cartridge, which had a powder charge contained in a copper case with a lead bullet seated on top. Within the rim of the case was a priming charge. This tiny .22-caliber cartridge, simply named the "rimfire," was to prove a landmark in self-contained metallic ammunition design and is still in production around the world, with literally billions having been manufactured subsequently. But it was of little use to the design of the larger rifles and despite the plaudits of the press, sales remained poor. With probably fewer than 3,000 rifles and pistols being manufactured in the years 1855–57, the Volcanic Repeating Arms Company continued to accumulate debts.

Crucially, during this time it had attracted a new major investor, Oliver F. Winchester (1810–80), and the name of the company was changed in 1857 to The New Haven Arms Company. Winchester may not have been a gunmaker, but he was an astute businessman and he acquired exclusive patent ownership of the Volcanic designs, as well as nearly 50 percent of the stock. At a stroke he became president, treasurer, and chief stockholder. By now, both Smith and Wesson had virtually ceased work on the long-arm side of the company, preferring to put all of their efforts into developing the pistol side of the business, as it seemed clear to them that this was where their future lay. They were materially helped in this decision by acquiring the vital Rollin White patent for a revolving cylinder that was bored through, enabling their new metallic cartridge to be used. It wasn't only pistols that attracted them, however, for both worked on developing their 1854 Flobert-based metallic cartridge, and they began producing larger calibers, heralding an entirely new era in the production of revolvers. In January 1857 they founded the Smith and Wesson Revolver Factory at Springfield, Massachusetts. In payment for handing over their patents to Oliver Winchester, they received the sum of $64,000 ($1,360,000/£874,000 today) and 2,800 stock shares; in addition, they entered into a gentlemen's agreement that the Smith & Wesson Company would not produce rifles, while Winchester would never manufacture pistols. It is here that their association with the rifles ended, but the story of the Winchester was only just beginning.

THE HENRY RIFLE

It seems fairly certain that by 1856 the foreman at Volcanic, Benjamin Tyler Henry, had already become heavily involved in the development work on the Volcanic systems, most specifically with the rifles. With Oliver Winchester now in sole control of the company, Henry was given the freedom to continue his experimental work on the rifles. One of his first tasks was to find a cartridge that would prove suitable. Henry wasn't a man to rest on his laurels and wait for something suitable to pop up, so in October 1856, having looked closely at Smith and Wesson's new rimfire design, he patented his own .44-caliber rimfire, finally doing away with the old Jennings/Smith and Wesson loaded-bullet concept. His invention was a rimfire-primed, copper-cased cartridge holding a conical 120- or 126-grain lead bullet propelled by 26 grains of black powder. The small charge produced a fairly low velocity of 1,125ft/sec, resulting in a short range of under 200yd with a very curved bullet trajectory. In modern terms, this performance would be considered suitable only for a handgun; this proved a limiting factor that would constrain the new rifle for many years, but it was a huge improvement over earlier designs. Each cartridge base was marked with an "H" to denote it was a Henry round. Nevertheless, by 1860, Henry had finished his work on the new rifle and it was ready for the commercial market.

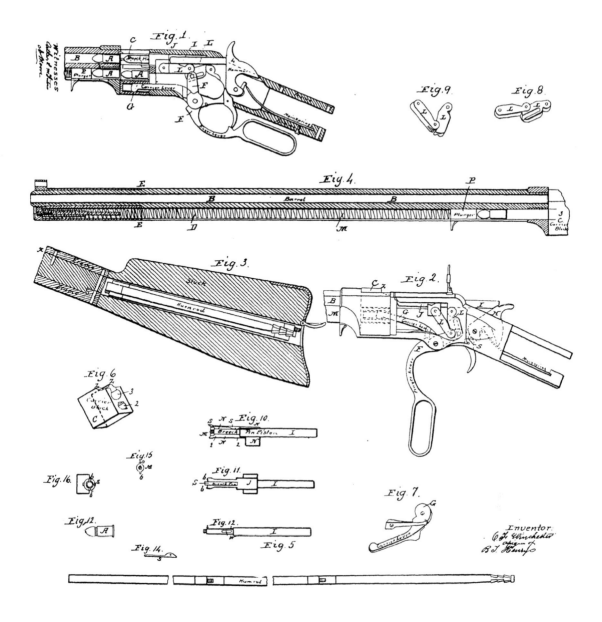

The Henry rifle patent of 1860 incorporated many of the features of the Jennings. (Author)

It was both distinctive and well-proportioned – with its handsome iron (later brass) receiver, neat lever/trigger guard combination, and octagonal barrel with full-length tubular magazine – and weighed 9.25lb. It worked in much the same way as the earlier Volcanics, with the advantage of having a cartridge extractor on the bolt-face. However, one down side of the mechanism was that there was no safety position. Once loaded, a Henry rifle would either have the hammer in the fully cocked position, or it could be lowered manually resting on the firing pin, which in turn was in contact with the cartridge. Henry appreciated this was a serious shortcoming, and subsequently all early sold rifles could be returned to the factory where a half-cock position was added to the hammer free of charge. It wasn't foolproof, but was certainly an improvement. The magazine held 16 cartridges, or 17 if the chamber was loaded. Allowing

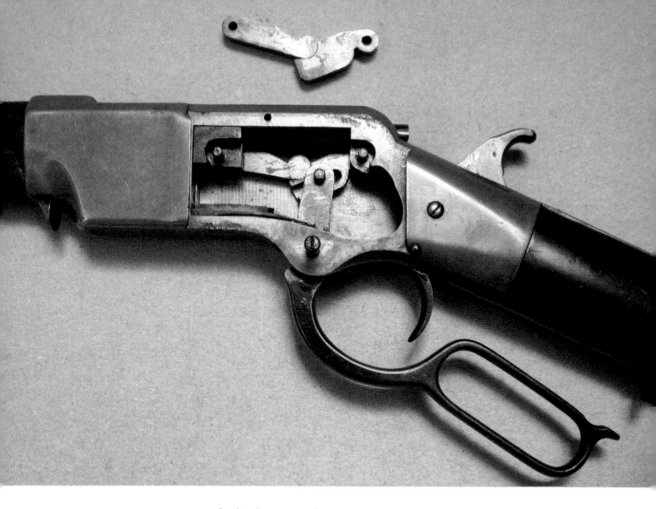

A left-side view of a Henry with the sideplate removed, showing the toggle action, with the left side plates of the link removed for clarity. Its simplicity was an advantage, but its relative fragility was to cause problems as the power of ammunition increased. Similar mechanisms were later adopted for the Maxim machine gun and the Borchardt semiautomatic pistol. (CC BY-SA 3.0/Hmaag)

for loading time, the Henry could shoot at 28 rounds per minute, which was considerably faster than other contemporary breech-loading repeaters.

Production was slow, as the New Haven Arms Company of Connecticut which had been formed in 1857 had a workforce of only 50 people, and when production of the Henry began in 1860, they were manufacturing fewer than 200 per month. It was, by the standards of the day, relatively expensive at $42 ($1,160/£720 today) at a time when a Springfield muzzle-loading military rifle was $12, but there was no doubt it could, in terms of sheer firepower, outshoot any existing rifle.

THE MODEL 1866

The year 1866 was to prove a seminal one in the history of the rifles, for not only did the company cease to be the Henry Repeating Rifle Company, becoming instead the Winchester Repeating Rifle Company, but the first Winchester design, the Model 1866, was introduced. This rifle, nicknamed the "Yellow Boy" because of its brass receiver, was the product not of Benjamin Tyler Henry, but of Nelson King, who had become the superintendent of the Winchester factory in mid-1866. King remedied the problems of the magazine tube by reversing the loading process. A hinged loading gate was placed in the right side of the receiver, allowing the

cartridges to be loaded from the rear. The magazine tube no longer required a full-length slot for the spring, as this was now fitted internally; the action of pushing the cartridges in simply compressed it automatically and the troublesome slot in the tube was now omitted. As King himself wrote:

> Within the tube I placed a follower and close the upper end of the tube by a plug … and between the follower and the lug I place a helical spring the tendency of which is to force the follower toward the … rear end of the tube … Through one of the [side] plates … I form an opening, through this opening, and when the carrier block is down … insert the cartridges, front first … the second cartridge pressing the first into the magazine, and so on. (Quoted in Wilson 1991: 25)

A wooden forend was fitted just in front of the receiver, which solved the problem of holding onto a hot barrel while also providing some protection for the magazine, for if a Henry was handled heavily the magazine tube could be dented, effectively cutting off the ammunition supply. In other respects, however, the Model 1866 shared much of its lineage with its predecessor. It was still chambered for the rather inadequate .44 rimfire, and used the inherently weak toggle-link action. Two versions were offered: a rifle with 24in barrel and a magazine capacity upped to take 18 cartridges, if one was pre-loaded in the chamber, and a carbine holding 14 cartridges with a 20in barrel. The early guns were roll-stamped with "Henry's Patent – Oct.16, 1860 / King's Patent – March 29, 1866." Interestingly, a statistical analysis of sales of the Model 1866 (Parsons 1966: 96) showed that the carbine outsold the rifle by almost seven to one. This was hardly surprising, as the barrel length had little impact on the range of the bullet (effectively 200yd), but it made a great difference to the practical ability of a rider to carry one in a saddle scabbard from where it could be withdrawn quickly. The shorter gun was also easier to point and aim, and at 7.4lb weighed almost 2lb less.

A Model 1866 "Yellow Boy" rifle, showing the contrast between the flat Henry receiver and the new design incorporating a loading gate and wooden forend. (Laurie Landau/Bob Maze)

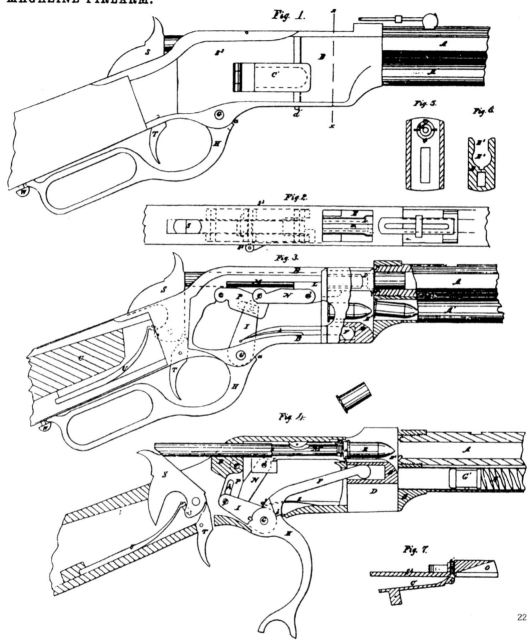

The patent document for the Model 1866 rifle. (Author)

THE MODEL 1873

Fortunately for the future of the Winchester rifle, by 1870 the science of metallurgy had moved forward somewhat and brass-cased centerfire ammunition was becoming more widely available. As sales increased, the company took the decision to move its manufacturing from Bridgeport back to New Haven, and in early 1871 the new facility was ready for occupation. In 1873 Winchester introduced the .44-40 centerfire cartridge, which became arguably the most widely used cartridge in America up to the beginning of the 20th century. Its 40 grains of black powder could propel a 200-grain lead bullet at 1,500ft/sec and higher velocities were quite feasible with hand-loading. As a result, in 1873 Winchester offered a new rifle, the Model 1873; it was, to quote contemporary sales literature, "built for the use of a longer ... centerfire cartridge, holding a charge of 40 grains of powder, with a sliding breech cover at the top to keep dirt and snow out of the lock."

Nelson's new gun was instantly identifiable by its steel receiver and sliding top cover, and for the first time it had an integrated safety sear which prevented accidental discharge of the rifle when the hammer was cocked. Savings in weight meant that it was now slightly less than 2lb lighter than the Model 1866. It also came in three barrel lengths: 20in, 24in, and a new musket length of 30in. The heaviest variant, the musket, weighed 9.3lb. In addition, round or octagonal barrels could be ordered. Uniquely, the carbine had a steel ring fitted to a lug on the left side of the receiver; this harked back to the sliders fitted to many cavalry rifles, enabling it to be secured to the saddle, or have a loop around the shooter's wrist, preventing accidental loss. The rifle sold for $27 and the carbine $24 ($439/£278 and $390/£247 today), although it is worth noting that these prices were often doubled by the time the guns had been shipped west.

Among other options offered were different grades of rifle, including silver or gold plating, engraving, set triggers and special carrying cases. A small but vital accessory was an all-in-one reloading tool which fulfilled all of the requirements of earlier tools, but combined them into a single, handy unit. In an era where many owners living in remote places had no

A Model 1873 with the right sideplate removed, the loading lever dropped and the action open. The carrier (the square steel block) is visible at center left; this would hold the fresh cartridge that had been pushed onto it from the magazine tube at bottom right. The sliding dust cover is visible on top of the receiver. (Laurie Landau/Bob Maze)

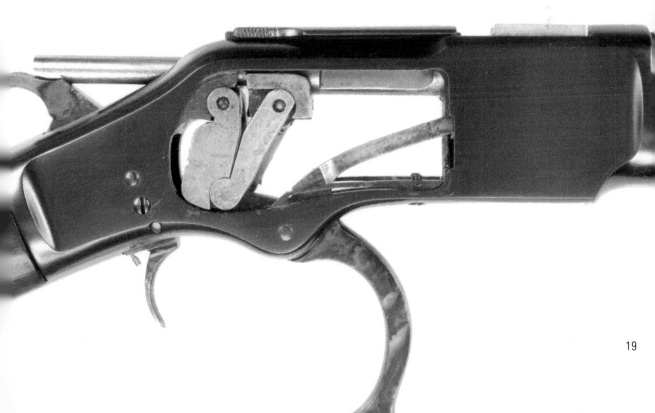

THE WINCHESTER EXPOSED

Model 1873 Winchester rifle

1. Buttplate
2. Buttstock
3. Hammer
4. Dust cover
5. Receiver
6. Rear sight
7. Front sight
8. Magazine tube
9. Forend protector
10. Forend grip
11. Magazine-tube spring

12. Cartridges in magazine tube
13. Finger-lever latch
14. Tang screw
15. Tang
16. Left rear link
17. Left front link
18. Breech-bolt face
19. Firing pin
20. Firing-pin spring
21. Extractor
22. Cartridge in chamber, just after firing

23. Carrier block
24. Carrier arm
25. Carrier-arm spring
26. Center link pin
27. Finger lever/trigger guard
28. Sear
29. Trigger
30. Sear/trigger spring
31. Safety-catch hook
32. Safety catch (outlined)
33. Mainspring

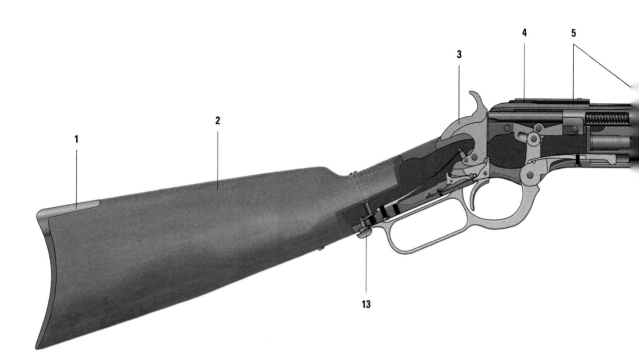

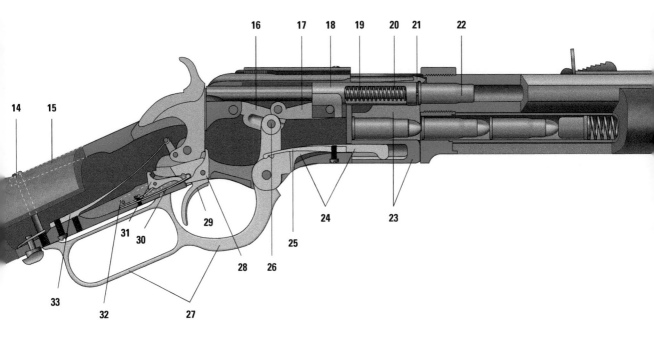

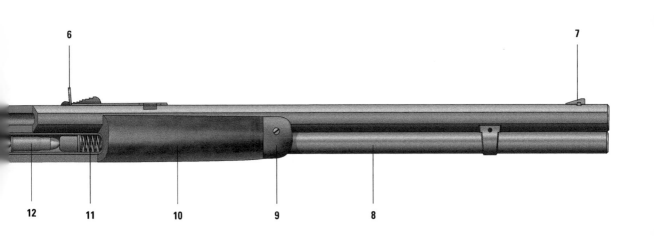

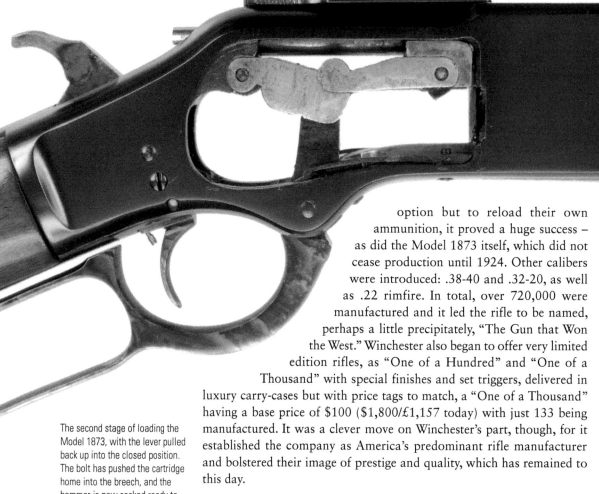

option but to reload their own ammunition, it proved a huge success – as did the Model 1873 itself, which did not cease production until 1924. Other calibers were introduced: .38-40 and .32-20, as well as .22 rimfire. In total, over 720,000 were manufactured and it led the rifle to be named, perhaps a little precipitately, "The Gun that Won the West." Winchester also began to offer very limited edition rifles, as "One of a Hundred" and "One of a Thousand" with special finishes and set triggers, delivered in luxury carry-cases but with price tags to match, a "One of a Thousand" having a base price of $100 ($1,800/£1,157 today) with just 133 being manufactured. It was a clever move on Winchester's part, though, for it established the company as America's predominant rifle manufacturer and bolstered their image of prestige and quality, which has remained to this day.

The second stage of loading the Model 1873, with the lever pulled back up into the closed position. The bolt has pushed the cartridge home into the breech, and the hammer is now cocked ready to fire. In terms of strength, it is little different from the Henry. (Laurie Landau/Bob Maze)

THE MODEL 1876

The problem with any rifle was that their owners needed one gun that was all things to all men; they were purchased for self-defense, hunting, law enforcement, and every other purpose that one could conceive of for a firearm. The limitations of having just one relatively small caliber to accomplish all of this was quite apparent to Winchester, and his introduction of other, smaller cartridges for the Model 1873 did little to ameliorate the issue. At the first-ever world's fair, the Centennial Exhibition held in Philadelphia between May and November 1876, the Winchester Company introduced a new model, which they fervently hoped would redress the situation. Indeed, the 1876 Centennial took the exhibition by storm, winning it a citation from the judges in the 1877 "Souvenir of the Centennial Exhibition" as the "best magazine rifle for sporting purposes yet produced."

The problem facing the engineers at Winchester had been in producing a mechanism that could take the longer and more powerful cartridges that

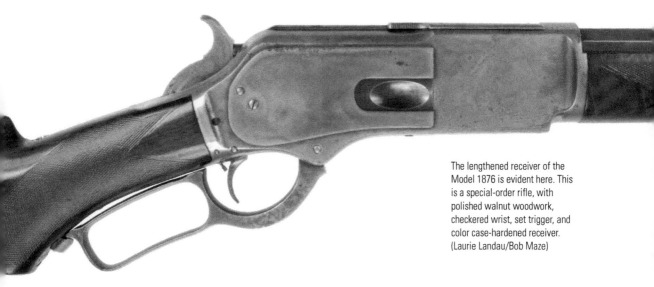

The lengthened receiver of the Model 1876 is evident here. This is a special-order rifle, with polished walnut woodwork, checkered wrist, set trigger, and color case-hardened receiver. (Laurie Landau/Bob Maze)

were appearing almost daily. They needed to produce a rifle that could hold its own when pitted against other, newer makes of lever-action rifles – such as Bullard, Whitney, and Marlin – that were capable of handling the larger cartridges. The only way to accomplish this was to beef up the bolt and toggle mechanism and lengthen the receiver, which was increased by 1.5in. This made it possible to handle a new Winchester cartridge, the .45-75-350. This was a bottlenecked .45-caliber bullet, weighing 350 grains and propelled by 75 grains of black powder that provided about the same energy as the Government .45 cartridge and a velocity of around 1,300ft/sec. The new cartridge reduced the capacity of the magazine, the 28in rifle now holding 12 rounds, and the 22in carbine nine rounds. The Model 1876 sold well and due to popular demand, two new cartridges were brought out in 1879, a .45-60 and .50-90 Express, then later a .40-60. In fact, ammunition production was rapidly becoming a major part of Winchester's inventory, for the firm had developed a reputation for manufacturing very high-quality cartridges. Some idea of the scale of this can be gleaned from the fact that between May 1874 and April 1875 Winchester produced for a Turkish military contract over 120 million .45-caliber Martini-Henry cartridges and 80 million .577in Snider.

The Model 1876 also appealed to a different breed of shooters, those who hunted big game in Africa, for the new calibers were perfectly capable of bringing down the largest of African animals – rhino, elephants, Cape buffalo – and in the Americas they could comfortably deal with grizzly bears, buffalo, and elk. Many high-profile figures used the new models, including the larger-than-life Theodore Roosevelt (1858–1919), and this helped materially to market the Winchesters far more effectively than advertising. As a result many European hunters began to carry the larger-caliber guns, and in total some 64,000 were produced. These rifles carried both of King's patents as well as the "Model 1876" designation on the upper tang, and had distinctive color case-hardened receivers.

JOHN BROWNING AND THE "PERFECT RIFLE"

Despite increasing sales and an expanding product line, there lay within the design of the Winchesters a fundamental weakness. Once the breech-block was locked in place, the toggle action relied on machined studs to take the pressures generated in the breech when firing. All would probably have been well had not a French chemist named Paul Marie Vieille (1854–1934) invented a new type of propellant in 1884. Aside from the smoke it

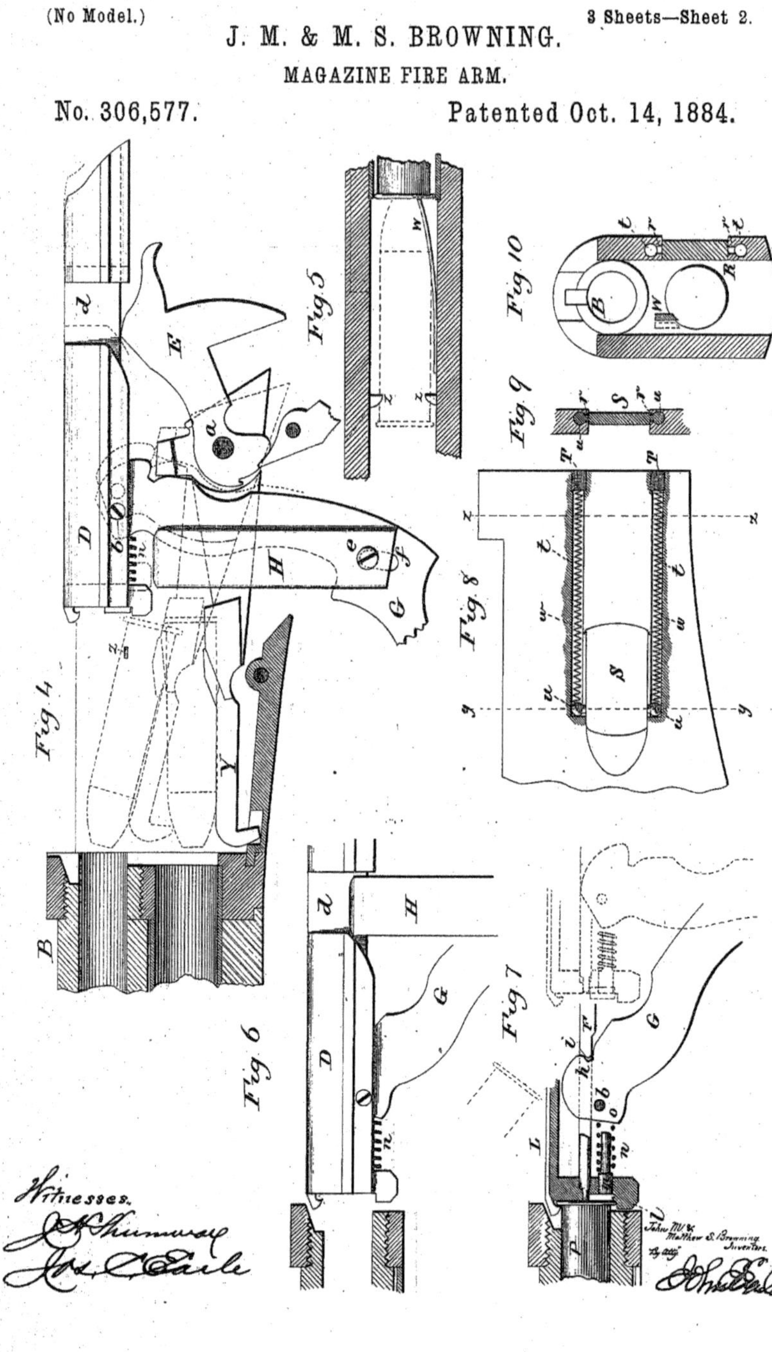

(No Model.)
3 Sheets—Sheet 2.
J. M. & M. S. BROWNING.
MAGAZINE FIRE ARM.
No. 306,577.
Patented Oct. 14, 1884.
Fig 4.
Fig 5
Fig 6
Fig 7
Fig 8
Fig 9
Fig 10
Witnesses.

The employment of John Browning by Winchester to improve the designs was a watershed in the history of the company. The 1884 patent shown here shows the method by which he strengthened the mechanism of what was to become the Model 1886 rifle. (Author)

produced and the acidic fouling it left behind in firearms, the greatest limiting factor with gunpowder was its slow burning rate, which resulted in low pressures and correspondingly low velocities, requiring large charges to counteract it. Vieille produced "Poudre B" (white powder) made from 68 percent nitrocellulose gelatinized with ether and paraffin. The resultant chemical was safe unless compressed, very moisture-resistant, and produced almost no smoke on discharge. Even better, it generated far higher breech pressures due to its fast rate of burn, typically 10,000lb per square inch higher in a .30-caliber cartridge than gunpowder. The problem this posed for the older-model Winchesters was that the new high-velocity ammunition could and did break the mechanisms, shearing the pins and occasionally sending the breech-bolt flying backward, with unpleasant results. It was clear that a new mechanism was required that was capable of safely handling the smokeless ammunition that was becoming increasingly popular from the mid-1880s onwards.

Winchester needed a solution and turned to a quiet genius of a gunmaker, John Moses Browning (1855–1926), probably the most significant and influential firearms designer in history. Browning and his Mormon brothers were men of great simplicity and astonished fellow engineers with the primitive tools they used for their design work: foot rulers, calipers, spirit levels, a protractor, and design sketches done on pieces of scrap paper were their stock in trade. Indeed, there did not exist a single drawing board in the workshop, nor was there ever a blueprint produced by them. John Browning was able to visualize in three dimensions and the brothers' ethos was that whatever they manufactured, they promptly went out and shot, putting their designs to the ultimate test. In fact, Browning had been working for the Winchester Company for some years, having produced a successful falling-block rifle in 1879. Winchester had wisely bought the patent rights and had been marketing this very popular model with great success. After a meeting with Browning in 1883 Thomas Grey Bennett, Winchester's president (Oliver Winchester had died in 1880), purchased for $8,000 ($188,000/£120,000 today) the rights to the falling-block design, as well as the first manufacturing rights of any new designs from Browning. Bennett was a very clever self-made businessman, who had enlisted in the Union Army in 1860 as a private and ended the war as an infantry captain. If he had one flaw, it was that he was no engineer and this resulted in a distrust of untried technology, as would become painfully evident in later years.

In engaging Browning, Bennett provided two things. First, Bennett gave Browning a financial freedom that he had never had before, enabling him to continue working on his designs to the eventual benefit of Winchester Repeating Arms. Secondly, Bennett secured for the company the future manufacturing rights to whatever the best engineering brain in the business was likely to produce. From Browning's point of view, the arrangement was perfect, for he understood only too well the risks that a company the size of Winchester's was taking when it decided to manufacture a new model. Three-quarters of the designs the company bought from Browning never went into production but, as Browning himself observed:

Bennett knows what he is doing. I sell him a gun – the '86 for instance. He pays a lot of money for it, and has a big investment in plant and materials. It would be a serious blow to him if someone should come out with … a gun of the same general type. I'm just building some protective fences … that what these guns are that he buys and never expects to make – fences. (Browning & Gentry 1987: 92)

It was a partnership that would endure for 20 years, although the relationship remained largely secret, for unlike Henry and King, Browning's name never appeared on any of the rifles.

THE MODEL 1886

What Winchester really needed next was an action capable of safely handling the pressures generated by the new smokeless ammunition, and it seemed that the falling-block design was the answer. There was nothing new in the concept and it dated back in its most simple form to the removable breech-blocks used in medieval cannon. More recently, it had been used most successfully by Sharps in their rifle and since the end of the Civil War many big-game rifle manufacturers had utilized the mechanism. It was, like the best inventions, both simple and foolproof. The action was a single piece of steel that dropped downward in machined grooves when the lever/trigger guard underneath the rifle was pivoted forward. This gave easy access to the chamber, and after a cartridge was inserted the lever was lifted upward, closing the block and locking the chamber. Once closed, the receiver effectively became one single piece of steel, making it literally unburstable. It could and did handle the most powerful of ammunition with no problems aside from the shooter's physical ability to deal with the resultant recoil. This was something the old Winchester design simply was incapable of doing, regardless of how much it was strengthened, unless it was made so massive as to be unusable.

Providentially, Browning had been working on a lever action that incorporated a falling-block mechanism, and in May 1884 he patented his new design, for which he was paid the then huge sum of $50,000 ($1,110,000/£700,000 today) by Winchester. Because of his agreement with Bennett this meant that over the next two years the company gained not only the patent and manufacturing rights of the new gun, the Model 1886, but 11 other

Two land claimants in Guthrie, Oklahoma Territory, pose for the camera in 1889. The man on the left leans on a Model 1886 Winchester, while the seated man holds a ubiquitous hammer shotgun. (University of Oklahoma, Western Library)

designs including the Model 1885 single-shot rifle and the iconic Model 1887 shotgun.

Browning's Model 1886 Winchester still retained its trademark lever action, but the toggle link was replaced by a vertically sliding breech-block, actuated by unlocking the lever and dropping it down; it also incorporated a rear-locking bolt for strength. The carrier still picked up the cartridge from the tube magazine in the traditional manner, but when the lever was closed, the bolt moved forward as the breech-block slid upward in its machined tracks and it then solidly locked the action shut. It enabled the rifle to chamber virtually any cartridge, although it was best suited to the mid-range ones such as .45-70 and .50-110. There were carbine and musket versions offered as well, with the usual expensively finished special-order rifles available from the factory, but by far the most popular was the rifle chambered for the .45-70 Government cartridge, and over 160,000 Model 1886s were sold until the end of production in 1935.

THE MODEL 1892

Emboldened by the success of the new gun, Bennett once more approached John Browning and requested that he look at the now aging Model 1873 rifle with a view to upgrading it. A rival to the Model 1886 wasn't what he wanted; what was needed was more like a strengthened version of the popular older models that could handle smokeless loads. The need to come up with a better design was imperative, because by the early 1880s several rivals had begun producing good alternative lever-actions. Marlin, Whitney-Kennedy, Colt Burgess, and Savage were making good-quality rifles, and all were taking valuable sales from Winchester. Additionally, many of these models were now capable of shooting smokeless ammunition. Attempting to use the higher-pressure loads in the old Winchesters was not a safe practice, and in desperation Bennett told Browning that he would pay him $15,000 ($351,000/£226,000 today) if he could have a working example at New Haven within two months. Never one to resist a challenge, Browning's response was businesslike and utterly typical: "I will have the rifle in your hands within thirty days for twenty thousand or I will give it to you" (quoted in Browning & Gentry 1987: 142).

Browning was better than his word and he excelled himself by having a working prototype sitting on his workbench in Ogden, Utah, only two weeks later. The Model 1892 was really a

Browning's 1891 patent for the Model 1892 rifle. (Author)

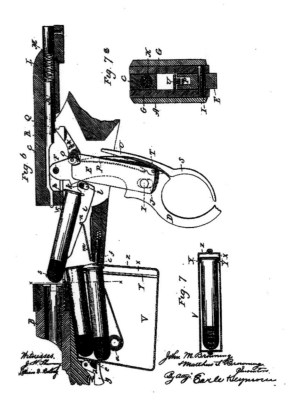

(No Model.)   5 Sheets—Sheet 5.
J. M. & M. S. BROWNING.
MAGAZINE GUN.
No. 465,339.   Patented Dec. 15, 1891.

The Model 1892. This was outwardly similar to the Model 1894, with sliding locking lugs, visible at the rear of the action, but it was better-suited to the range of smaller calibers that were so popular. (Laurie Landau/ Bob Maze)

scaled-down version of the Model 1886 rifle; that it would prove successful was almost a foregone conclusion, for demand was huge. The Model 1892 was produced in a vast number of variants: sporting rifle, carbine, musket, and a novel take-down model that unlocked at the breech. They were mostly chambered for the lighter cartridges such as the .32-20, .38-40, and of course the ubiquitous .44-40. The Model 1892 proved a huge financial success, with over 1 million being sold. It would gain considerable fame (and sales) from being the Winchester model used most frequently on film and television.

THE MODEL 1894

"The ultimate lever-action." The receiver of the Model 1894, showing the length required to chamber the new .30-caliber cartridge. The top of the sliding-block reinforcing added by Browning can be seen in front of the hammer. (Laurie Landau/ Bob Maze)

Never a man to rest on his laurels, Browning's next design was the Model 1894, which differed little visually from its predecessors and had originally been designed to chamber the two most popular black-powder cartridges, the .32-40 and .38-55. Browning's revised mechanism still retained the toggle design, albeit a stronger one than those in the earlier guns, but the carrier was fixed to the lever and lifted the cartridge into position at an

angle to the breech. As it closed, the bolt was pushed forward, chambering the cartridge; the breech was locked by a heavy, vertically sliding block that was mortised into the rear of the receiver, making it capable of handling far higher pressures than the earlier types. The carbine was also light and handy, weighing a modest 6.6lb. Within a year of its introduction, a higher grade of steel was introduced which permitted the action to handle the .30-30 Winchester cartridge, introduced in 1895.

This was a seminal design, being America's first lever-action rifle capable of handling the new small-bore, high-velocity, smokeless cartridges. The .30-30 bullet diameter was actually a very modern design; its .308in diameter and bottleneck cartridge design enabled a velocity in excess of 1,970ft/sec, using the original 160-grain bullet, and eight rounds could be chambered in the rifle, or six in the carbine. Far higher velocities were possible with different bullet configurations, and to say that the introduction of this rifle and its cartridge were watersheds in firearms technology is something of an understatement. The .30-30 has subsequently become the yardstick cartridge by which all others are judged in terms of performance, and despite its moderate size it was capable of bringing down large game at normal hunting ranges of up to 200yd. The Model 1894 became synonymous with the .30-30 caliber and some measure of its success is that even today it is still the most widely used rifle for hunting in the Americas, and it is still in production. As the 1894 Winchester catalogue flatly stated: "No repeating rifle system ever made will appeal to the eye and understanding of the rifleman as this will." These were prophetic words indeed, for the total of rifles made to date now exceeds 7,500,000 and special editions have been made, including a gold-inlaid and engraved example produced for the Paris Exhibition in 1900 by Tiffany and Company of New York.

THE MODEL 1895

By the 1890s the successive waves of settlers and hunters heading west had all but ceased. As the railroads extended ever farther towards the west coast, so too had civilization steadily crept across the continent. The buffalo had virtually been wiped out and farming had taken over much of the Great Plains. The Native American tribes had been ruthlessly subdued and there was little requirement, or enthusiasm, for the lives of brutally hard self-sufficiency of 30 or 40 years previously. No longer did items ordered from the East take weeks to arrive and cost a small fortune. Such hunters and trappers as still worked could purchase ammunition in virtually any nearby town, and there was little requirement for them to carry powder, bullets, and cases which had to be loaded in the field. Besides, there was no doubt in anyone's mind that the latest breed of high-velocity ammunition performed far more efficiently than the old black-powder cartridges. In the 1870s no hunter who wanted to reach old age would have considered tackling a bear with a .30-caliber rifle. By the 1890s it was a standard hunting caliber for virtually any game in North America. While there was no doubt that many older rifles were still being

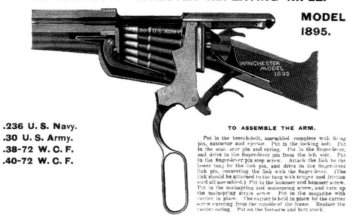

THE LATEST WINCHESTER REPEATING RIFLE.

MODEL 1895.

.236 U. S. Navy.
.30 U. S. Army.
.38-72 W. C. F.
.40-72 W. C. F.

TO ASSEMBLE THE ARM.

Put in the breech-bolt, assembled complete with firing pin, extractor and ejector. Put in the locking bolt. Put in the sear, sear pin and spring. Put in the finger-lever, and drive in the finger-lever pin from the left side. Put in the finger-lever pin stop screw. Attach the link to the lower tang by the link pin, and drive in the finger-lever link pin, connecting the link with the finger-lever. (The link should be attached to the tang with trigger and friction stud all assembled.) Put in the hammer and hammer screw. Put in the mainspring and mainspring screw, and turn up the mainspring strain screw. Put in the magazine with carrier in place. The carrier is held in place by the carrier screw entering from the outside of the frame. Replace the carrier spring. Put on the fore-arm and butt stock.

A drawing of the compact magazine and receiver of the Model 1895. It bears all the hallmarks of Browning's design genius and little relationship to earlier Winchesters. One of the cartridges listed is the .236 US Navy (also called the 6mm Lee), which despite being the first rimless cartridge adopted by the US military was never a popular commercial loading, and commercial production in .236 caliber ceased by 1903. (Author)

used with black-powder loadings, it was also obvious that the days of black powder were numbered.

Browning had been particularly interested in advances made in European firearms technology through the late 19th century, in particular the almost universal adoption throughout Europe's armies of magazine rifles. Even the United States, always glacially slow to decide upon its service arms, had accepted the Krag-Jørgensen rifle into service in 1892. By now, one could be forgiven for thinking that Winchester Repeating Arms pretty well had the marketplace sewn up as far as lever-action rifles were concerned, but Browning was an inveterate inventor and could not leave an idea to fester. He had been considering the limitations of the tubular magazine for some time, with its vulnerability to damage and the need to use flat- or round-nosed ammunition. This was due to the potential risk of a pointed bullet striking the primer of the cartridge in front of it if a rifle was dropped or carelessly handled. With the conical or flat-nosed lead bullets normally chambered in black-powder cartridges this was unlikely, but the smokeless cartridges were increasingly using pointed jacketed bullets, which were far more liable to cause a problem. Browning went back to the concept of using a rear locking bolt of the type seen in the Model 1886 rifle and produced what was to become Winchester's last lever-action rifle, the Model 1895. Barrels were available in 24in, 28in, and 30in lengths and the standard finish was deeply blued. In an attempt to lighten the rifles, the receivers had distinctive fluted sides, although very early examples were flat-sided and today these are the rarest encountered.

In a break with tradition, the Model 1895 featured a box magazine that held, depending on the caliber of ammunition, four or five rounds; it was produced in a number of popular calibers, including .30-40 Krag, .30-03, .303 British, and several specific Winchester loadings, including the most powerful ever chambered by a lever-action, the fearsome .405. This was a good big-game cartridge, but showed up the weaknesses of the design, for the modest weight of the rifle (9lb) was little different from that of the earlier models, which of course were chambered for much less powerful cartridges. The relatively light weight of the rifle, allied to a sharply angled stock, transferred punishing recoil to the shoulder when used with heavy loads. In fact, the .405 cartridge proved the extreme limit for safety in a lever-action rifle and later attempts to chamber larger big-game cartridges using smokeless powder failed, the design never being developed any further.

USE
North, South – and West

THE HENRY IN THE CIVIL WAR

The outbreak of hostilities between North and South in 1861 provided Oliver Winchester with an unexpected chance to try to interest the US Army in his new rifle. Although there were at least 11 functioning breech-loaders available to the military, only two were repeating rifles, the Model 1855 Colt Revolving Rifle and the Model 1860 Spencer rifle. Aside from the competition, for both Henry and Winchester the biggest stumbling blocks to the acceptance of their new rifle was in actually getting the guns to the Ordnance Board for testing. There were so many designs appearing (excluding muzzle-loaders the author has counted 20 models of breech-loading rifles and carbines introduced during the war years) that it required some form of personal influence to ensure that the rifles were properly examined, something both Colt and Spencer were able to achieve. The second stumbling block was the Chief of Ordnance himself, Brigadier General James W. Ripley, whose attitude towards repeating arms could reasonably be described as cool. He declared in a written report to the Secretary of War in December 1861 that, "One must be aware of the great evil … in regard to … the vast variety of new inventions. I regard the weight of the arms with the loaded magazines is objectionable, and also the requirement of special ammunition rendering it impossible to use … with ordinary cartridges or with powder and ball" (quoted in Williamson 1952: 33).

Perhaps history should not judge Ripley too harshly, for there were certainly serious logistical problems affecting the Union Army where weapons and ammunition were concerned during the war years. Not only were there several different standard-issue calibers for muzzle-loading rifles, but also variations for cavalry carbines, as well as a plethora of new ammunition appearing for the new capping breech-loaders – and this

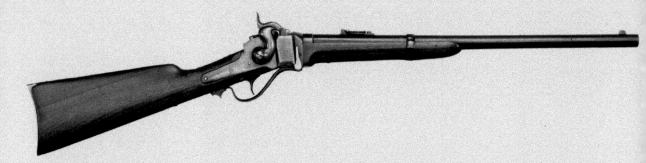

ABOVE A Model 1863 Sharps carbine. After the Civil War, many were converted to .50-caliber centerfire, and they continued to be used in the fighting between the Army and Native American tribes until the adoption of the Springfield Model 1873 rifle. Many thousands were purchased as war-surplus for as little as $2 apiece and were carried west. Special-order rifles, chambered for the big .50-90-caliber and .50-110-caliber Sharps ammunition, were largely responsible for providing the firepower that enabled the hunters on the Great Plains virtually to wipe out some 60 million buffalo by 1880. Production of the Sharps ceased in 1881, by which time over 120,000 had been manufactured. (© Royal Armouries XII.2480)

The Henry's rivals

Despite the fact that the Sharps was a single-shot, percussion rifle, it proved to be an enduring weapon during the Civil War and in the turbulent years afterward. Its falling-block breech design was unbreakable and it held up well to the hardships of service use. A carbine for cavalry use was ordered by the US Government in 1853. Coincidentally, these were manufactured by Robbins and Lawrence, and during the Civil War were issued to 82 regiments. A 30in-barreled military musket was later supplied in large numbers. Its .52-caliber combustible cartridge was very powerful and it was accurate at ranges in excess of 1,000yd. At 9.5lb it weighed 2lb more than the carbine. A special version, ordered for

the 1st Regiment of Berdan's Sharpshooters during the Civil War, was the first rifle to be adopted officially for sharpshooter use by any country.

Colt's Model 1855 Revolving Rifle, despite the company's reputation for its fine six-shot revolvers, was not exactly a technological leap forward. The original carbine of 1838 was simply an enlarged Paterson revolver which had several failings, the most serious of which was also common to the revolvers in that it was structurally weak, having no top strap. As a result, in 1855 Colt's factory superintendent, Elisha Root, patented a solid-frame design, with a side-hammer; it also had an improved cylinder-locking mechanism. Colt trialed it before a board of Army officers,

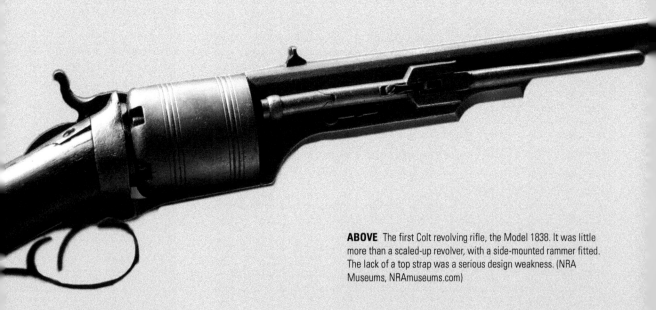

ABOVE The first Colt revolving rifle, the Model 1838. It was little more than a scaled-up revolver, with a side-mounted rammer fitted. The lack of a top strap was a serious design weakness. (NRA Museums, NRAmuseums.com)

ABOVE A Model 1860 Spencer rifle. It used a lever-cocking action, but unlike the Henry, the Spencer employed an internal revolving breech-block/carrier design that was incredibly strong. Lowering the lever dropped the breech-block down then rotated it backward, allowing the cartridge to be pushed onto the carrier; pulling the lever back rotated the breech-block/carrier, pushing the cartridge into the chamber and simultaneously raising the breech-block into the firing position. The shooter had to cock the hammer manually, but all seven shots could be fired in 10–12 seconds. (© Royal Armouries XII.2690)

where it was reported that: "… during the testing, the firing was deliberate. They were not cleaned, and sufficient time was only allowed for them to cool when hot. They worked smoothly and easy. None failed to go off, and the cylinders showed less deposit than usual" (US National Archives Record Group 74.145).

Consequently, Colt secured his first US Government order in October 1856. Of course, testing was one thing, but the reality of field use was quite another, and the Colts soon developed a nasty reputation for being dangerous due to chain-fire of the cylinders. This was not unique to them, of course, and could occur with any front-loading black-powder cylinder arm, when grains of powder accumulated in crevices of the frame and cylinder. The result was that on firing, the ignition of one chamber ignited the loose powder which in turn chain-fired the other cylinders simultaneously. This resulted at the very least in an extremely shaken shooter with a burned left hand, which was the one normally gripping the forend just underneath the cylinder. In the worst cases, men lost their sight or much of their left hands, and so poor was the reputation of the Model 1855 that during the war the soldiers of at least one Union regiment, Berdan's Sharpshooters, said they would mutiny if they were forced to use the Colt, stating that even the muzzle-loading Springfield was a better arm. Neither were the Colts particularly cheap, at $45 each, inclusive of bayonet, but the Union Army still ordered 4,600 in total during the war years. Proper cleaning normally reduced the problem to almost nothing, but it was usually exacerbated by lack of maintenance when in the field.

Arguably the most sophisticated repeating rifle available by the start of the war was the Model 1860 Spencer. It was the result of years of experimentation by Christopher Miner Spencer (1833–1922), an engineer and inventor who had, coincidentally, worked for Samuel Colt at one time. He conceived the idea of a repeating rifle that used a unique removable, seven-shot tubular magazine seated in the butt of the rifle. He patented the design in 1860, and submitted an example for inspection during field tests carried out in June 1861 by the Army Board of Examination. The Spencer fired a rimfire cartridge, of .56 caliber, which was modified after testing to become a necked .56-52 in order to increase velocity and improve its range. It caused quite a stir, the Superintendent, John A. Dahlgren – himself a man of considerable gunmaking experience – noting in his report to the Chief of Naval Ordnance that:

> An arm was presented here merely for examination which operates so well that I am induced to bring it to your notice. The mechanism is compact and strong. The piece was five hundred times in succession … there was but one failure to fire. The mechanism was not cleaned and yet worked throughout as at first. Not the least foulness [was] on the outside and very little within. I can recommend that a number of these pieces be introduced for trial in service. (NARG 74.145)

The military certainly took him at his word, for during the next four years the Union Army and Navy ordered 11,472 Spencer rifles, during which the price dropped from $41 to $35 per rifle. Spencer improved the mechanism with a second patent in June 1862 that covered improvements to the breech design, the guns providing reliable service through the Civil War and beyond.

An iconic photograph of the 10th Illinois Volunteer Infantry, five of whom are holding Henrys for the benefit of the camera. The photo, by Mathew Brady, was taken c.1862. At this date, such a weapon would have been a great rarity on the battlefield. (NARA)

didn't include any of the new metallic cartridges required. At least one Union regiment, fighting for its life, opened boxes of arsenal-supplied ammunition to find that the bullets supplied for their .58-caliber rifles were of .62 caliber, and soldiers frantically whittled them down with knives so they could be used (Pegler 1998: 172). If there was one thing Ripley didn't need it was yet another caliber with all of the logistical problems that entailed. Although he proved a major stumbling block to the concept of introducing repeating firearms, or indeed any modern firearms to the US Army, there were ways to circumvent him. Winchester personally presented several Henrys to prominent politicians, including President Lincoln and the Secretary of the Navy, Gideon Welles, who were doubtless very gratified, but it resulted in no movement towards Government orders or even field trials.

However, the Union Army's ever-expanding requirement for firearms was pressing, as it doubled, then tripled in size. In December 1861, the Henry and Spencer were both trialed; unsurprisingly, the Henry outshot the Spencer, firing 187 shots in 3 minutes 36 seconds and managing to discharge a full magazine in 10.8 seconds (Wilson 1991: 11). Admittedly, the distance it was fired at was moderate, 348ft, which was due to the lack of power of the Henry round, but although it impressed those present, it

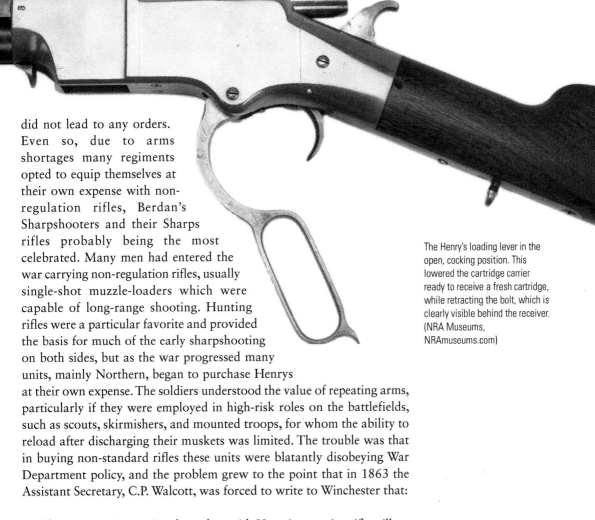

did not lead to any orders. Even so, due to arms shortages many regiments opted to equip themselves at their own expense with non-regulation rifles, Berdan's Sharpshooters and their Sharps rifles probably being the most celebrated. Many men had entered the war carrying non-regulation rifles, usually single-shot muzzle-loaders which were capable of long-range shooting. Hunting rifles were a particular favorite and provided the basis for much of the early sharpshooting on both sides, but as the war progressed many units, mainly Northern, began to purchase Henrys at their own expense. The soldiers understood the value of repeating arms, particularly if they were employed in high-risk roles on the battlefields, such as scouts, skirmishers, and mounted troops, for whom the ability to reload after discharging their muskets was limited. The trouble was that in buying non-standard rifles these units were blatantly disobeying War Department policy, and the problem grew to the point that in 1863 the Assistant Secretary, C.P. Walcott, was forced to write to Winchester that:

> Those companies arming themselves with Henry's repeating rifle will not be allowed to retain them in the field. If you choose to arm and equip a whole regiment at your own expense, or the regiment chooses to arm itself, it will be accepted with the condition that it shall be at liberty to use its own arms and equipments exclusively. (Quoted in Williamson 1952: 28)

In other words, the units concerned had to pay for their own ammunition and not expect any assistance from the US Government. The Spencer, which had been adopted in considerable numbers, was proving very effective in the hands of the soldiers, being tough and mechanically simple. The magazine was easily inserted into the stock and could be easily kept clean, although forgetting to lock it into place often resulted in the loss of the loaded tube, but it could be replaced in seconds.

Because the Henry was only officially issued in very small numbers, mostly to mounted units, accounts of its use are sparse. Possibly the most oft-repeated comment about the Henry was as the result of its use by eight

The Henry's loading lever in the open, cocking position. This lowered the cartridge carrier ready to receive a fresh cartridge, while retracting the bolt, which is clearly visible behind the receiver. (NRA Museums, NRAmuseums.com)

companies of the 1st District of Columbia Cavalry, to whom the Federal Government had supplied 800 Henrys. The guerrilla chief, General John Mosby (1833–1916), commented that "I do not care for the common gun, or for Spencer's seven shooter, but as for these guns that they can wind up on a Sunday, and shoot all week, it is useless to fight against them" (quoted in Wilson 1991: 14). In fact, the Henry probably saw more action with or against irregular troops as it did in the formal battle-lines. Many guerrilla units and raiders armed themselves very heavily, each carrying three or four revolvers and a Spencer or Henry rifle, for reloading a musket on a moving horse was a difficult feat, although not impossible. The repeaters gave mounted men a huge firepower advantage. In the border areas, where towns were likely to face the depredations of Confederate or Union raids, many opted to arm themselves with the Henry, which sometimes paid dividends. A Union man, Captain J. Wilson, lived in a heavily disputed area of Kentucky and was well aware of the possibility of becoming a target for Confederate sympathizers. He had taken the precaution of erecting a small log cabin opposite his house, in which he stored revolvers and his Henry rifle. One evening, as he was eating with his family, seven Confederate guerrillas rode up, burst into his house, and began firing indiscriminately with their revolvers. One bullet actually smashed the water glass his wife was holding, but it says much for the revolver-shooting ability of the men that they actually hit no one. As the family fled, Wilson sprang to his feet and shouted: "For God's sake, gentlemen, if you wish to murder me, do not do it at my own table in the presence of my family" (quoted in Williamson 1952: 38). It says much about the social mores of the time that this resulted in a heated moral debate between the guerrillas about the best course of action, and they agreed to go outside to shoot Wilson! As the published account then explained, Wilson's forethought in equipping his shed with firearms was to save his life.

> The moment he reached his front door he sprang for his cover and his assailants commenced firing at him. Several shots passed through his hat and more through his clothing but none took effect upon his person. He thus reached his cover and seized his Henry rifle, turned it upon his foes and in five shots killed five of them; the other two sprung for their horses. As the sixth man threw his hand over the pommel of his saddle the sixth shot took four of his fingers off, but the seventh shot killed him; then starting out, Capt. Wilson killed the seventh man with the eighth shot. (Williamson 1952: 38)

It comes as no surprise that Wilson, who later became a captain in the Kentucky Cavalry, was instrumental in ensuring that the unit was wholly armed with Henry rifles. He had much to be grateful to them for. By coincidence, or possibly because of its popularity in Kentucky, there are several accounts of the Henry's effective use as the fighting ebbed and flowed through the state.

> The Henry Rifle is regarded in Kentucky as the most effective weapon known, and some most astonishing things have been accomplished

with it; among these we mention one: Whilst the gallant Col. Netter was raising his regiment of Kentucky Volunteers at Owensboro, Ky., he sent fifteen of his men armed with this rifle on a scout; these men were attacked by two hundred and forty rebel soldiers in an open lane, where there was no timber for shelter, and the fifteen Union soldiers, armed with the Henry, successfully repulsed and drove from the field the two hundred and forty assailants. This unparalleled feat could not have been accomplished with any other arm known to us. Respectfully, R.K. Williams, W.W. Gardner. (Quoted in Cleveland 1864: 179)

The Henry magazine unlatched with the spring fully forward, at which point it could be loaded with cartridges. (Laurie Landau/ Bob Maze)

Although the majority of Henrys had been issued to cavalry units, plenty of infantry also carried them on both sides. A total of 68 Federal units had Henry rifles although not necessarily every man was equipped with them, and some 16 Confederate regiments carried them. It is interesting to speculate from where they purchased their guns, but it is more than possible that many were bought over-the-counter by Southern sympathizers in the North and smuggled South.

Such was the need for weapons that in 1863, despite their misgivings, the Federal Government reluctantly began to purchase Henrys, albeit in fairly small quantities. However, its adoption was hindered by a design shortcoming that apparently had not been apparent when tested. In order to load a Henry, the hinged front section of the magazine underneath the muzzle was twisted to one side, providing access to the magazine tube and enabling the cartridges to be inserted. Before this was done, the shooter had to push a thumb-piece that projected from a slot on the underside of the receiver to the front of the magazine tube. This compressed the entire magazine spring in the forepart of the magazine tube. Once all of the cartridges were loaded, the front section was swiveled back in alignment with the magazine tube and the thumb-piece released, enabling the compressed spring to exert pressure on the cartridges, ensuring they fed reliably onto the carrier in the receiver. The problem was that in muddy conditions, the slot under the tube and the front of the magazine tube accumulated mud and debris, preventing the spring from being compressed and effectively stopping the rifle being reloaded. In addition, there was a similar problem affecting the open top of the receiver, as no cover had

been designed that could prevent dirt and debris dropping into it. There was no immediate remedy for these shortcomings, though, and all Winchester could do was to issue instructions with the rifles that it was imperative to keep the receivers and magazines free of dirt.

There was little doubt that the Henry did not fare well as a military rifle during the war, as evidenced by the fact that the Government purchased 94,000 Spencer rifles but a mere 1,731 Henrys. While this was a disappointment to Winchester, there was some consolation that civilian sales were good, with around 13,000 Henrys being purchased between 1862 and 1866. The first few hundred were iron-framed, but to ease production by cutting material costs and reducing machining times, the rest were brass-framed. The octagonal barrels and round magazines were problematic to make, being very costly to manufacture, each barrel being milled from a single bar of steel, with flanges of metal having to be bent around a mandrel to create the round magazine tube. Then of course, there was the loading problem which could not be addressed without major re-design of the magazine system.

The open ejection port on the top of a Henry. The bolt can be seen to the right, and the smallness of the cartridge can be gauged from the size of the aperture. The open nature of the port was also a problem as it permitted dust and dirt to enter. (Laurie Landau/Bob Maze)

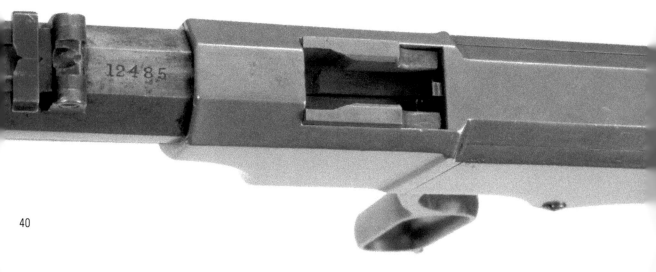

THE US ARMY IN THE INDIAN WARS

Because of the scale and impact of the Civil War, it is often overlooked that there was still a continuing running battle along the Western frontier between the Army and indigenous tribes. Initially, the forts had been largely denuded of men because of the demands of the war in the East, and those that were left struggled to keep the Native Americans in check. Raiding parties would descend suddenly on timber-cutting and foraging wagons, routine patrols, and reinforcements coming to the forts. So serious was the situation that in 1861 the US Secretary of State for War, William Seward, was forced to allocate more troops to the frontier, taken mostly from the Army of the Ohio, as the westernmost force was then known. Although the troopers were armed with issue Sharps or Spencer carbines, many privately purchased Henrys appeared as well, frequently in the hands of officers and civilian contractors who were more likely to be able to afford them. There were several notable battles during the Civil War years between the Native Americans and Army, in particular the Sioux tribes, but ownership of a Henry did not automatically confer immortality, as this 1893 account from *Harper's Magazine* showed:

> George W. Northrup became orderly sergeant of Company C in Brackett's Battalion of Minnesota Cavalry, which for a time was part of the Fifth Iowa Cavalry in the Army of the Cumberland … Brackett's Battalion was ordered to the frontier in 1864 to aid in suppressing the Sioux, who had risen against the whites in 1862, and against whom an ineffectual expedition had been sent in 1863 … No one knows what he said; but the Sioux recognized him, and determined to slay the handcart man. The wild Indians of the plains who had no guns shot at him with arrows. George had a sixteen-shooter, and Brigadier-General Miner Thomas told me that he saw three Indians fall under his rapid fire. I doubt not that every shot took effect. But at last, pierced by three arrows, Northrup fell dead.

This lesson was much reinforced during the Indian Wars, in the years roughly between 1860 and 1890, for while the Native Americans had revolvers and rifles, including some repeaters taken from white men, they continued to arm themselves with fearsomely accurate self-bows, which with their 50–60lb draw weight could discharge a killing arrow every three or four seconds out to 200yd, which was almost beyond the accurate use of a Henry rifle. The Native Americans could also use the bows to drop arrows almost vertically down onto prone targets, something no firearm was capable of doing. During the bitter fight on December 21, 1866, later known as the Fetterman Massacre, two Henry-equipped Army scouts were killed by arrows, as were almost all of the other 80 troopers who died. It was estimated that some 40,000 arrows were fired into their position by concealed warriors and neither the Henry-armed scouts, nor the regular soldiers, had any defense against the highly efficient Stone Age technology.

A year later, in August 1867, it appeared as if history was to be repeated when a wagon party of 29 soldiers and civilians came under ambush from an estimated 600–800 warriors in Wyoming. These soldiers were armed

ABOVE A Model 1884 infantry-issue "Trapdoor" rifle. (© Royal Armouries XII.2572)

ABOVE A Model 1896 Krag rifle. The Krag-Jørgensen weighed 7.5lb and had a 30in barrel. Magazine capacity was five rounds of the .30-40 cartridge. (NRA Museums, NRAmuseums.com)

The Army's choices: the "Trapdoor" and the Krag

The Springfield Model 1873 rifle was universally known as the "Trapdoor," because of its hinged breech-block design. It was the brainchild of Erskine Allin (1809–79), Master Armorer at Springfield, but owed much to earlier rifles, such as the British Calisher and Terry and the American Morse. The US Army wanted a method by which it could convert, simply and cheaply, the thousands of .58-caliber muskets in store to cartridge use, and Allin's Model 1866 rifle – using a thumb-operated cam latch at the rear of the breech-block – was simple to operate and convert. It was designed to chamber a primitive type of centerfire cartridge, the Benet-primed .50 caliber. After some teething problems it was modified and first saw action at the "Wagon Box" fight during the war against Red Cloud in July 1867, where it acquitted itself well. An improved version, the Model 1870, was subsequently introduced in both rifle and carbine form, but the old .50-caliber cartridge suffered from reliability issues and the new Model 1873 chambered the Government's new .45-70 cartridge. This latest rifle had a 32.6in barrel and the carbine a 22in barrel, the rifle weighing in at 8.4lb. They could be fired at a rate of ten rounds per minute, a rate more than double that of a muzzle-loader; but in the humidity of the West, there were often problems with extraction, as verdigris on the cartridges acted like glue, sealing them in the chamber when the rifle was fired. In part, this was blamed for the failure of Custer's 7th Cavalry to hold off the Native Americans during the battle of the Little Bighorn (June 25–26, 1876). It was, however, a robust and simple rifle and up to 1892, when its service life ended, some 700,000 were manufactured.

The Krag-Jørgensen was a minor milestone in American military rifle history, being the first bolt-action magazine rifle to be adopted. It was designed by two Norwegians, Ole Herman Krag (1837–1916), an army officer and firearms designer, and Erik Jørgensen (1848–96), a prominent gunsmith. They adopted a turning-bolt mechanism, based on the successful Mauser principle, but used an unusual side-mounted box magazine that enabled loose ammunition to be fed into the magazine via a hinged flap. Closing the flap, in theory, forced the cartridges into line ready for chambering, and was supposed to be faster than using a conventional stripper-clip. After 15 years of prevaricating, testing numerous breech-loading rifles, in 1892 the US Government eventually chose the Krag, but after complaints by other manufacturers the trials were rescheduled to be run once more the following year. Again, the Krag came out on top and in 1893 the Ordnance Board authorized Springfield Armory to begin production of the weapon as the Model 1894.

In combat it was found that the Krag did not perform well in humid climates such as Cuba and the Philippines, and during the Spanish–American War of 1898, the Spanish soldiers' Mauser – which chambered a higher-velocity 7mm ammunition – both out-ranged and out-shot the Krag. One serious defect of the Krag was that the side-mounted magazine proved to be slower to reload than the Mauser's, and there were also problems with the Krag's hinged door unlatching, accidentally emptying the magazine. The rifle stayed in service for only nine years, although in that time some 700,000 were manufactured; it was replaced by the Springfield Model 1903, which proved to be an excellent rifle.

Despite the terrible massacre of General Custer's force at the Little Bighorn on June 25–26, 1876, whose men were armed with single-shot rifles, there continued to be little interest from the US Army in adopting repeating rifles, mostly due to the basic design concept of the lever-action. It was always going to be weak and the tubular magazine prone to jamming. Besides, the Army was wary of fast-shooting weapons that could consume huge quantities of ammunition. In reality, though, most of the real criticism was leveled at the poorly performing 44-40 cartridge. All attempts to get the US Government to adopt the Winchesters during the Indian Wars failed, mainly due to the lackluster performance of the available cartridges when compared to the issue .45-caliber ammunition. There was also strong competition from outside of the United States from bolt-action designs that chambered far more

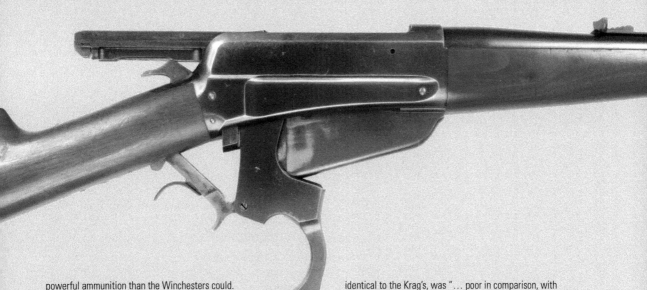

powerful ammunition than the Winchesters could.

However, in the wake of the outbreak of the Spanish–American War of 1898 some 10,000 Model 1895 rifles in .30-40 Krag caliber were ordered by the US Board of Ordnance, but the war ended prior to their delivery. An interesting by-product of this was that 100 rifles were subsequently supplied for field trials during the Philippine–American War (1899–1902). They were tested by the 33rd Volunteer Infantry Regiment against the issue Model 1892 Krag rifle; the report makes interesting reading, for it was highly critical of the mechanism of the Model 1895, which was: "Prone to jamming due to dirt and sand … it is difficult then to clean when in the field." Furthermore, the accuracy of the cartridge, despite its being

identical to the Krag's, was "… poor in comparison, with range much reduced to the service arm. The Krag-Jørgensen is a superior military arm in almost every respect" (US Congress Annual report of the Chief of Ordnance, 1898. Serial No. 3752). As an unexpected by-product of this canceled contract, the rifles were then sold to an American arms dealer who shipped them to Cuba, from where they found their way to Mexican rebels led by Pancho Villa, who used them against the American forces during the Mexican Revolution (1910–20).

ABOVE The right side of the Model 1895 showing the much-strengthened action. Despite its ability to handle smokeless cartridges, it was still prone to jamming due to the ingress of dirt and the lever action was considered too vulnerable for it to be used as a military arm. (Laurie Landau/Bob Maze)

LEFT An interesting image from c.1880 of an Army scout (center left, standing) surrounded by Apache scouts, all armed with "Trapdoor" Springfields. The Army officer at right holds a Springfield carbine. (Arizona Historical Society)

with breech-loading Springfields, which were certainly an improvement on the old muzzle-loaders, and their speed of firing materially slowed down the Native Americans' initial assault. But it was the repeating rifles that really proved their worth during the long day of fighting as the war party crawled nearer and nearer in an attempt to rush the soldiers' position, a crude breastwork of logs. After the death of the senior officer, a civilian named D.A. Colvin took control. He was probably armed with a Henry, although it may possibly have been a new Model 1866. Colvin's effective use of it was described by another participant, Finn Burnett:

> I don't believe there is another man living ... who has killed as many Indians in a day as Colvin did on the occasion of the hayfield fight. He was armed with a sixteen-shot repeating rifle and he had a thousand rounds of ammunition. He was a dead shot and if he missed an Indian in that fight none of us ever knew it. He fired about three hundred shots that day ... most of his shooting at distances of from twenty to seventy-five yards, it was almost impossible for him to miss. He was shooting steadily from nine-thirty in the morning until five o'clock in the afternoon. And the ground where he was stationed was literally covered with empty shells from his rifle. (Garavaglia & Worman 1985: 122)

The white men lost three dead and half a dozen wounded; Indian losses are unknown.

SETTLERS IN THE INDIAN WARS

Early accounts of civilian use of the Henrys were usually reported in the local press, and two of the earliest encounters between Henry-armed settlers and Native Americans were published nationwide. The normal tactics of Native Americans when faced with white men armed with muskets involved creeping forward to just outside accurate shooting range, then using one warrior to tempt the soldiers or settlers to open fire. Once their single-shot muskets were discharged, the Native Americans would launch a mass charge, hoping to overwhelm the white men before they could reload. Although the revolver had helped to reduce the risk somewhat, it was primarily a last-ditch, short-range weapon, and during the immediate postwar expansion of the West, while most settlers had revolvers, their rifles were mainly single-shot muskets.

If range was not the main asset of the Henry, then rapid fire was, for the introduction of the repeating rifle brought a whole new dimension to countering Native American tactics. One of the first accounts of Native Americans meeting Henry rifles face-to-face was published on November 22, 1865, in Denver's *Rocky Mountain News*, in which the Native Americans commenced a textbook attack in 1865:

> One morning the two young ex-soldiers had hardly begun the day's operations when they saw the enemy approaching and knew they were in for it. Some forty warriors dismounted at a distance, approached to

Prospector and trapper J.F. Steward, pictured in 1871 with his Winchester Model 1866 in Glen Canyon, Colorado. (NARA)

nearly gun range, lay down … and began deliberately to creep in, spreading out to surround their doomed victims. Once in range they began to expose themselves for an instant … but always doing so two at a time in the hope of getting the guns of both whites empty simultaneously. One of the youths … said to his companion: "As soon as they get near enough, we'll fire together. They'll rush us the moment we both fire: and then'll be the time for you and me to do some shooting!" It happened precisely as he foresaw. With full magazines they agreed to bring on the decisive charge. At the word of one, both fired … and the moment the two flashes and puffs of smoke were seen simultaneously a whole band of Blackfeet sprang to their feet and dashed yelling in on their supposed unarmed and helpless victims. But those two guns kept on firing! Shot after shot kept pouring from the guns over the low log breastwork and … man after man of their

Spreading the word

By mid-1862, the Henry rifle had become commercially available and civilian sales had begun to look quite promising. The problem for the makers of any type of firearm in the mid-19th century was in finding effective methods by which to advertise. There was no form of national media and traveling across country from east to west could take a month, making sales trips painfully slow. There did exist a network of frontier gun dealers – some quite large affairs, such as Albright and Kitteridge, who were on the edge of the frontier in St. Louis, and Gove and Rood in Denver – but there were dozens of others, mostly small affairs where the owner was also the working gunsmith. In a move that was later to be copied by other manufacturers, Winchester realized that if his rifles were freely available for testing by anyone that might possibly be inclined to spread the gospel, then it would materially help sales. Resultantly, gunshops were encouraged by Henry to allow prospective purchasers to try the guns for themselves. Often this simply meant handing them a box of cartridges and opening the back door and this worked tolerably well, as the results were rapidly spread by word of mouth.

However, the best method was via newspapers or popular magazines, such as *Harper's* and *Scribner's*, or specific periodicals such as *Forest and Stream*. They were by far the most widely read and easily available form of communication, and all were encouraged to test the guns. Some were unrealistically enthusiastic; one testimonial – from A.A. Vanwarmer in 1863 – stated that the Henry could be fired at the rate of three shots per second, which was about triple the actual rate of fire. He also made wild claims about the ranges that the .44 cartridge was capable of achieving: "I bought one of the first … Henry rifles sold here. I have carefully tested it … it is certain death at 800 yards, and a probable at 1,000. I lent it to a friend … after the shooting with the Enfield rifle, and amateur operations with the Sharp's rifles etc., my friend beat them all" (quoted in Garavaglia & Worman 1984: 262).

The editor of the *Louisville Journal*, a wealthy and very pro-Union gentleman named George D. Prentice, was also eulogistic in his praise for the rifles in the issue of July 14, 1862, commenting, not untruthfully, that: "One man, with this weapon is equal to fifteen armed with ordinary guns. It may be loaded for a week at the bottom of a river, and, if taken out will then fire with as much certainty as if it had been kept perfectly dry all the time." In a sideswipe at the Colt revolving rifles, he also added, "It is remarkably simple … and is utterly free from the objection sometimes urged against other repeating rifles that two or more charges are liable to be fired at once." In fact, in this he was basically correct, for it was precisely these abilities which appealed to shooters who were frustrated by the inability of muzzle-loaders to be kept reliably charged for any length of time and which were so slow to reload. So enamored of the Henry was Prentice that he ordered several hundred and sold them to customers who were loyal to the Union. This was not uncommon, for it was particularly noticeable that the majority of early sales were to those living in the border states – West Virginia, Tennessee, Arkansas, and North Carolina – who were tormented by renegade raiding parties, or under constant threat of attack from bandits or disaffected Native American tribes.

Civilian sales of the Model 1866 began in early 1867, although interest was initially slow, in part due to a reluctance on the part of Winchester actually to advertise his new rifle. Even in 1868, the sole Western agents for the model were Freund Brothers, a large company that specialized in supplying miners, trappers, and anyone else with a desire to head West. By 1868, other companies finally began to offer the rifles, and from this date sales began to increase quickly. But the

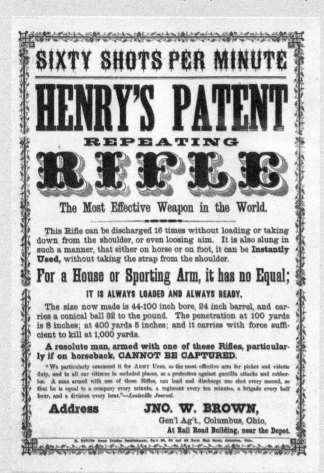

LEFT A Henry advertising flyer, within which there were some claims that could be regarded as questionable. (Author)

rifle was only a half-solution to the problem of lack of range and power, and many Westerners refused to buy one on the grounds that it simply wasn't powerful enough. This was quite a reasonable objection, as a Sharps rifle with its .52-caliber combustible cartridge was perfectly capable, in skilled hands, of being fired out to 1,000yd and of felling a buffalo at 500yd, and the additional problem of misfires still dogged Henry ammunition. How serious this was is difficult to estimate, for all rimfire ammunition suffered to a greater or lesser degree from poor distribution of the primer compound within the rim. Often removing the cartridge and reinserting it in a slightly different position within the breech solved the problem, although on a Henry or Winchester, failure to fire simply meant ejecting the uncooperative round and chambering a fresh one. But many shooters disliked the unreliability of the cartridges and their lack of stopping power, particularly on potentially dangerous game such as buffalo. This was an important factor in influencing sales, for the majority of Winchesters were being sold in the expanding Western territories, where the reliability of a firearm was of paramount importance.

RIGHT As demand for the rifles grew, the Winchester Company began to offer special models, with custom engraving, deluxe stocks and carry-cases. This Model 1866 is typical of the simpler style of engraving that was available. Some rifles were real works of art and cost the equivalent of a year's wages for a working man. (Author)

number fell shrieking or silent in the prairie grass as the deadly and unheard-of continuous firing blazed steadily at them; and at a range so short ... few if any of the young rifleman's bullets missed. But as they fled the guns kept at them and only a few escaped un-hit. Reloading their magazines the youths ... ended the desperate work by leaving no wounded alive ... and dragged the whole number to a heap at a distance beyond rifle range of their fort, that the survivors might return and contemplate the fatal results of their terrible encounter with weapons that obviously appeared never to need to be reloaded at all. From that day on no other attack was ever made upon the pair ... one of them I later knew ... told me, meeting an Indian whom he had reason to believe had to have been one of the survivors of the fight, the brave, with a face of horror, exclaimed "Spirit guns! Spirit guns!" and was off as fast as his pony could gallop.

This account is interesting for several reasons. Most significantly, both men were ex-soldiers, disciplined enough to hold their fire until the Native Americans were suitably close; they were also experienced enough to draw the Native Americans within their effective killing zone, as the writer comments specifically on how near the attackers were to them. As a Henry had a maximum accurate range of not much more than 200yd, the Native Americans must have launched their charge at well under that distance – even for experienced soldiers it took a steady nerve and good shooting to stop a determined charge, even with the benefit of a repeating rifle. It was an early experience for the Native Americans of just how deadly the repeaters could be, and there is little doubt that word spread quickly among the tribes about the incredible new rifle.

In 1866, a young adventurer named Edward Ordway was heading west by means of the Bozeman Trail, accompanying a wagon train within which was a shipment of new firearms, among them some crates of Henry rifles. Ordway was not particularly enamored of it, commenting: "It was short ranged and could do but little damage beyond two hundred yards, but it was as near mechanically perfect as any machine gun could be made, and in the hands of the men of the day sixteen shots could be fired with astonishing rapidity" (Ordway 1925: 153). When Pawnee scouts were sighted, the wagons corralled in a textbook circle, the horses unharnessed in the center and the wagon wheels being chained together. The defenders lay underneath, each resting his rifle on the wheel spokes to steady his aim. These wagon-men were old hands and many were armed with muskets, but they sensibly held their fire as the Native Americans circled closer and closer.

That they [the Pawnee] got no reply from the old muzzle-loaders ... was positively a puzzle they could not solve, but kept drawing a little nearer until perhaps their patience became exhausted. They made a simultaneous dash on all sides, and coming within the limits of the rifle range the Henrys began to play a tattoo the like of which they had never heard before. To say the Indians were astonished at the storm of lead that met them would be but a weak expression. It was but a very

few minutes after we began to fire ... they were scurrying away towards the shelter of the hills ... They let us alone while in their territory. In less than an hour the train was rolling along as merrily as though nothing had happened. (Ordway 1925: 149–51)

That the new rifles were starting to provide a level of security beyond simply that of firepower was evident, for in both instances the men mention that they were subsequently left alone by the Native Americans, who did not wish to tangle with the new guns. A similar party traveling downriver in a Mackinaw boat that same year were also mostly armed with Henrys, which they had already put to good use when ambushed on the river by a war party of Sioux. At 150yd the party opened fire: "Not more than ten minutes elapsed before every one of them had disappeared. Their fearful death howl, however, assured us that our fire had not been in vain" (Langford 1893: 241). Proof that having the new rifles was worth the cost was soon evident, for the same group shortly came upon a party of steamboat-men cutting wood for the approaching vessel:

> These men were armed with Hawkins [Hawken] rifles, which being muzzle-loading, were greatly inferior to the breech-loading cartridges then in use. We warned them of the danger, but with their energy and enterprise they possessed also the courage and recklessness of all pioneers. Poor fellows! The chances were too strong for them, for only a few days afterwards a body of Sioux Indians came upon them. They made a desperate defense but were overpowered and every one of them massacred. (Langford 1893: 352)

One of the biggest weaknesses of the Henry was in the design of the tubular magazine. This photograph illustrates the front of the magazine tube as the shooter pushes the brass tab forward to compress the spring prior to unlatching the front of the tube. If choked with dirt this became impossible. (Laurie Landau/Bob Maze)

IN NATIVE AMERICAN HANDS

The Native American tribes who fought the encroaching white men may have been lacking technical expertise, but they were not slow when it came to adopting the most modern firearms technology available. As soon as they began facing white men armed with firearms, they realized that they were at a serious disadvantage, particularly when their chosen means of attack was so reliant on close-quarter fighting. The Native Americans inevitably began to acquire guns and it was not long before the white men were on the receiving end of their own technology. For many years it was believed by historians that most Native American tribes predominantly used muzzle-loaders, which were simple to mend and use, with a few captured or traded breech-loaders, but in the wake of more research it has become clear that this was clearly not the case. From the first introduction of the Henry rifle, Native Americans wanted to acquire them and they did so by any means possible, sometimes via unscrupulous white traders who would swap them for gold or furs, or simply by killing their original owners. An 1881 report assessing an Apache attack in Arizona noted that:

> This party was armed, as in fact were nearly all the hostiles in Mexico, with the latest models of Winchester magazine rifles, a better arm than the single shot Springfield with which our soldiers and scouts were armed. The Indians obtained their arms from settlers and travelers they killed, or purchased them from white scoundrels who made a business of selling arms, ammunition, and whiskey to Indians. (Quoted in Davis 1929: 59)

Neither did it take long for the new technology to filter west. Members of the Sioux tribes were carrying .44-40 Winchester Model 1873s, only two

A photo of Tzi-Kal-Tzn of the Nez Perce tribe, holding a Henry rifle. A close look at the wrist of the gun shows that it appears to have been repaired with a brass plate. The stocks were easily split if handled carelessly, and this was a common method of repair on the frontier. Tzi-Kal-Tzn was reputedly the son of the explorer Captain William Clark and an indigenous woman. (Montana Historical Society)

years after the rifles had first become available commercially. Allowing for the time it took for anything to reach the Midwest, this was a remarkably short time span. One reason often cited for Native American reluctance to use the repeating rifles, or indeed any of the new cartridge firearms, was the difficulty they supposedly had in obtaining ammunition. However, there is much contemporary evidence to prove that when they wanted them, cartridges were freely available. An Army sergeant who served in Texas wrote: "There is a belief common among people … that the Indians fought solely with bow and arrow, but in all my Indian fighting, which amounted to seven pitched battles, besides several skirmishes, I have always found them well equipped with good guns and plenty of ammunition" (quoted in Garavaglia & Worman 1985: 363). This is borne out by records that have survived from the Government trading posts that were spread across the Indian agencies. One recorded that in six months they had sold 2,000 .44 rimfire cartridges for Henry and Model 1866 rifles. Another Crow Agency noted that in 1873 over 20,000 rimfire cartridges had been sold. A trader named Manuel Garcia noted that: "I got two [buffalo] robes from the other buck for three boxes of Henry cartridges" (Garcia 1967: 151–53).

Of course, many of these purchases were for legitimate hunting, but a considerable number would be turned against the white men over the coming years. The Native Americans were also ingenious when it came to reloading empty cartridges, although the .44 rimfires posed them a real problem, as it was almost impossible to get any primer compound into a used case without fairly complex machinery. However, with the introduction of centerfire

Spotted Hawk, a Montana Cheyenne warrior, is pictured in full battle regalia with a well-worn Model 1886 rifle. (Montana Historical Society)

Indian Wars, 1875 (overleaf)

It was not often that American soldiers faced an enemy that was armed with more modern weapons than they possessed, but frequently during the long years of the Indian Wars, US soldiers found themselves on the receiving end of their own technology. In 1868 the US Army authorized the issue of 50,000 Allin-designed, Model 1868 "Trapdoor" Springfield rifles. These single-shot guns were chambered for the new .50-70-caliber centerfire cartridge, and they continued in Army use until the end of the Indian Wars. Although powerful and accurate, in the type of fighting commonly practiced by the Native American tribes, the soldiers were often at a disadvantage, as Native American tactics called for them to close with the soldiers and then rush them, which showed up the dangerous shortcoming of the single-shot rifles. For the Native Americans, use of repeating rifles was an ideal solution, as they could put up a heavy covering fire while both moving forward and attacking. The Apache warriors depicted here are armed with a mixture of Henry and Winchester Model 1866 and 1873 rifles.

The Apache Chief Geronimo and several Chiricahua braves. The two on the left are carrying what appear to be Model 1873 carbines, while the third man has a Springfield cavalry carbine. Geronimo, at right, holds a Springfield infantry musket. (Arizona Historical Society)

ammunition they could reload almost anything. Colonel Richard Dodge, who had considerable experience of Indian fighting, wrote:

> He [the Native American] buys from the trader a box of the smallest percussion caps, forces the cap into the shell until it is flush. Powder and lead can always be obtained from the traders; or in default of these, cartridges of other calibers are broken up, and the materials used in reloading his shells. Indians say ... that the shells are frequently reloaded 40 or 50 times. (Dodge 1883: 417)

Across the entire frontier, the Indians continued to do their best to equip themselves with the latest Winchesters, obtaining Model 1876 and Model 1892 guns with their more potent cartridges. But the times were changing very quickly and resistance to the overwhelming numbers of whites was clearly becoming futile. It was a particularly cruel irony that the last pitched battle, at Wounded Knee on December 29, 1890, was between the 7th Cavalry and elements of the Hunkpapa and Lakota Sioux, some of whom had fought at the Little Bighorn. Many of the young Indians had Winchester carbines, which were short enough to hide under their blankets. When the Army ordered the men to surrender their weapons, the situation deteriorated very quickly, as interpreter Philip Wells recounted:

> I heard someone on my left exclaim, "Look out! Look out!" I saw five or six young warriors cast off their blankets and pull guns out from under them and brandish them in the air. One of the warriors shot into the soldiers, who were ordered to fire into the Indians. I looked in the

direction of the medicine man. Captain Wallace was killed at this time while standing in front of his troops. A bullet, striking him in the forehead, plowed away the top of his head. (Wells 1948: 26)

After the unequal fight, which left 146 Indian men, women, and children dead on the battlefield, the Indians' weapons were gathered up. It proved to be an eclectic mix of firearms and, significantly, most of them were noted later as being repeating rifles, predominantly Winchesters. The dead Ogalalla Medicine Man was photographed for posterity, his Winchester next to him.

ON BOTH SIDES OF THE LAW

Of course, it was not simply Native American warriors who clashed with the settlers, for the new territories were a breeding ground for robbers, bushwhackers, and renegades. Throughout most of the vast area west of the Missouri, there was virtually no law, and the few Army forts that existed were often established in the middle of nowhere, taking days to reach. Through the 1860s and 1870s, where law needed to be enforced, it was usually done by a voted-in sheriff aided by a posse of available citizens with an experienced local tracker; engagements were usually short and bloody, often with summary justice being handed out. Although the first Transcontinental railroad had been established between Omaha and California in 1869, neither the Southern Pacific nor the second Transcontinental were finished until 1883. During this time stagecoaches were the primary means of transporting people, goods, and particularly money to and from the farthest reaches of the West; by 1832 there were 106 routes from Boston alone. Although they could only carry light payloads, they were fast and often used for transporting gold or currency, which inevitably made them a prime target for robbers. Having a guard on board was obligatory, but armed only with a muzzle-loader or shotgun

An atmospheric photograph of Texas Rangers armed with a variety of Winchester Model 1873 carbines. The seated man fourth from the left has a special-order long-barreled rifle with pistol-grip stock. At least three of the rifles are saddle-ring models. Visible revolvers appear to be Colts, and all the men carry knives. (University of Oklahoma, Western Library)

The Dalton Gang, killed during their abortive raid on Coffeyville, Kansas, on October 5, 1892. The Winchester Model 1886 lying on the bandits was reputedly carried by Bob Dalton, second from left. (Kansas State Historical Society)

he was at a severe disadvantage in the event of attack by a determined gang, and most passengers traveled well armed.

Stagecoach companies began to issue Henrys early on, believing that it gave their passengers and cargo a better chance of survival. There are several instances of attacks being beaten off, not through the rifle's accuracy, but by its sheer firepower, as the *Rocky Mountain News* reported on July 22, 1867:

> The passengers on the stage from Denver this Monday last, were fortunate in their journey in having two guards armed with new repeating rifles, for when ambushed by a party of scoundrels the coach made good its escape by means of the fusillade of bullets rained upon the bad men who, considering their chances, decided that easier prey were to be found.

So often were the remote stagecoach staging posts the target of attacks that the employees were heavily armed with weapons, including repeating rifles; they turned the posts into self-contained forts, as a contemporary account described:

> Built of wood and stone are the stables and the ranche where the drivers and ostlers live. A little subterranean passage, about five feet by three, leads from the stables to the house. Another leads from the stables to a pit dug into the ground, about ten yards distant … [this] is roofed with stone supported by wood, and just on a level with the ground portholes open on all sides. Another subterranean passage leads to a second pit, commanding the other side of the station; while

a third runs from the corrale ... to the rear. In both houses many Spencer and Henry breech-loading rifles – lie loaded and ready to hand. During the three weeks we were in the neighborhood, the station was attacked twice. (Bell 1869: 32)

Sometimes the confrontation was even more personal than that. After the robbery of a stagecoach laden with gold leaving Nevada City in May 1866, the deputy, Steve Venard, armed with his Henry rifle, began to track the three robbers:

Venard crossed the bridge ... and came upon Jack Williams ... leveling a long .44 revolver. And at that instant, Venard's rifle leaped to his shoulder. Also at that instant, Venard saw Finn ... drawing a bead on him from the summit of the islet. Venard drilled Jack Williams ... through the heart. A flip of trigger guard and another half-ounce of lead was in firing position, just where Mr. Tyler Henry had once pledged Mr. Winchester it would be. The second shot, dispatched before the echo of the first had caromed off the cliffs ... spattered on the canyon wall, having entered Finn's skull below the right eye and toured his skull en-route. Bandit number three was doubling and twisting like a hare along the steep brush covered hillside. Venard's rapid shot all but winged him. The next shot out of the pursuing Henry explored his heart, sent his spirit winging and his person crashing downhill into the canyon. Three dead men, two of them still clutching cocked revolvers, and one live deputy. But – four expended bullets. The Henry must be getting old. Steve Venard was regretful. The stagecoach had been robbed at 4.30 ... the treasure was back in the express company keeping by two p.m. (Wilson 1987: 112)

Although a great improvement over the rimfire, the .44-40 was basically still a revolver cartridge, but if the Army had objections to it, they were certainly not upheld by the various law-enforcement agencies who took to the Winchesters with alacrity. In the early 1870s the Texas Rangers were mostly carrying Civil War-surplus Sharps carbines which were

Men of Canada's North-West Mounted Police, who were almost exclusively equipped with Model 1876 rifles. (Cody Firearms Museum)

chambered for the .50-caliber centerfire cartridge, but few were happy with the Sharps. For them range was not the issue, but rapid fire was, and the Model 1873 fulfilled their criteria perfectly. A Ranger named James Gillett saw one in a dealership in Austin, Texas, and was instantly smitten: "Ten men in Company D, myself included, were willing to pay the price to have a superior arm. I got a carbine number 13401, and for the next six years I never used any other weapon" (quoted in Garavaglia & Worman 1985: 216).

HUNTING

For the men working and fighting across the frontier, it seemed unarguable that there was a huge benefit to possessing a repeating rifle compared to a single-shot rifle, and in the ten years after 1865 repeaters were to become the most popular long-arm carried for self-defense. Of course, it was not only the need for protection that required the use of a rifle, for hunting was both a popular sport as well as a necessity, and as the Winchester models were gradually improved, they began to attract a greater following among sportsmen.

The eventual replacement in 1873 of the old, underpowered .44 rimfire cartridge with the .44-40 was one significant advance. Although it was ideal from the point of view of being compatible with the Colt (and many other) single-action revolvers, the plainsmen who hunted buffalo dismissed it as a toy and one hunter, P.C. Bicknell, wrote in 1874 that: "The Winchester is the laughing stock among these men, they would not take one as a gift if they had to use it" (quoted in Garavaglia & Worman 1985: 186). When hunting a less sturdy quarry, however, the rapid fire of the Model 1873 proved ideal. When James Schultz was hunting deer with a friend, he noted that "as each one leaped into the open of the trail, Eli fired at it with his '73 Model Winchester repeater. He fired three shots as fast as I could count them, with the result of three dead bucks lying within a yard or two of one another" (quoted in Garavaglia & Worman 1985: 185).

Jamming was a persistent problem with the lever-action rifles. Sometimes the cartridge rims caught at the rear of the magazine tube, and on the Model 1873 and some later models that chambered .44 ammunition great care had to be taken to avoid inadvertently loading the rifle with .45 Colt cartridges, which necessitated removing the sideplates to gain access to the cartridge carrier to remove the stuck cartridge. Like many others, hunter J. Mortimer

A view of a fine special-order Model 1886 with full-length magazine, rear tang peep-sight, hooded front sight, and high-quality checkered stock. (NRA Museums, NRAmuseums.com)

Murphy was not entirely happy with the rifle, stating that he was "Compelled to leave a buffalo hunt on two occasions" and that for shooting heavy game "the charge of powder that it carried was too small" (quoted in Garavaglia & Worman 1985: 186).

The problems regarding the underpowered ammunition were eventually rectified with the introduction of the Model 1876, which finally enabled hunters to use the larger calibers – notably the .45-60, .45-75, and .50-95 Express – to bring down even the biggest game. Traditionally, single or double rifles had been carried, as they were strong enough to chamber the cartridges required, but the Model 1876 and Model 1886 Winchesters finally heralded the more widespread use of lever-actions for hunting big game. A man with as much experience with the lever-action weapons as any person alive was Theodore (Teddy) Roosevelt, who was both extremely particular about the guns he used and very knowledgeable as well.

Frontiersman and hunter John Y. Nelson, who was to become the stagecoach driver in Buffalo Bill's Wild West Show. He always carried a Winchester Model 1873. (Author)

For long range work I use a .40-90 Sharps ... and a .45-75 half-magazine Winchester Model 1876. The Winchester is by all odds the best weapon I ever had, having killed every kind of game with it, from a grizzly bear to a big-horn. It is handy to carry ... and there is no recoil to jar and disturb the aim, while it carries accurately as far as a man can aim with any degree of certainty. For shooting the very large game of India and South Africa, much heavier rifles are undoubtedly necessary, but the Winchester is the best gun for any game to be found in North America. (Roosevelt 1885: 185)

Some animals in North America, such as bear, elk, buffalo, and cougar, were particularly hard to kill without using a heavy, large-caliber bullet; if the beast were wounded, the ability to reload and shoot again could mean the difference between life and death. In the bigger calibers the Winchester was also noted for its flat bullet trajectory, which made shooting at normal hunting ranges of perhaps 200yd far easier, as sights did not have to be adjusted. When two hunters in the Rocky Mountains in the 1890s were surprised by a foraging grizzly bear, the first raised his rifle, a .45-90 Sharps single-shot, and fired at the charging animal with little apparent

effect. Before he could reload, it rose up and swiped him with a massive paw, sending him flying to the ground. As it towered over him, his companion, armed with a Model 1866, fired three shots in as many seconds, hitting the bear in the head and killing it instantly. As the shooter later reported, "When he recovered from his injuries, my companion lost little time in exchanging his old single-shot for a new Winchester, and would carry nothing else from that date onwards" (Taylor 1932: 37).

With the increasing use of smokeless ammunition, the introduction of Winchester's big .405 cartridge in 1904 at last enabled them to meet on even terms the British hunting rifles that were primarily used for big game.

OPPOSITE Teddy Roosevelt photographed in 1885, looking every inch the hunter. His rifle is a Winchester Model 1873 De-luxe with half-magazine, shotgun-style stock, checkered woodwork, and monogrammed escutcheon, which is just visible on the butt. (Library of Congress)

"Little Sure-Shot" Annie Oakley with her much-favored Model 1892. Most of her shooting was done with .22 rimfires and she had several Winchesters provided to her free by the factory. She believed no other rifle could be chambered and fired as fast as the Winchester, although she also used the company's .22 pump-action. (Author)

The Model 1895 rifle, chambered for this cartridge, could take on any animal, notwithstanding its punishing recoil. Roosevelt, whose personal use of the Winchesters provided priceless publicity for the company, even had specially shaped stocks supplied by the factory, with 1.5in-thick rubber butt-pads attached to try to lessen the recoil, to little avail. Nevertheless, the fast-shooting rifles proved their worth when hunting lion in Africa:

> Right in front of me, thirty yards off, there appeared, from behind the bushes which had first screened him ... the tawny. Crack! The Winchester spoke, and as the soft-nosed bullet plowed forward through his flank the lion swerved so that I missed with my second shot; but my third bullet went through the spine and forward into his chest, down he came. (Roosevelt 1910: 232)

In fact, despite the input of John Browning, there was inevitably a physical limit to the strength of the action that could be practically fitted into the Model 1895, and it was to prove the apogee of the lever-action Winchesters. However, it was to see considerably more action in the hands of some of the world's armies.

FOREIGN MILITARY USE

It was not only the civilian marketplace that had been closely following the development of lever-action rifles. Several European governments expressed an interest in the Model 1866 rifles, and Winchester traveled to Europe in 1866 and 1867 to demonstrate his guns, but nothing came of it. Oddly, it was from much closer to home that the first substantial order was to come when Mexico placed an order for Winchester rifles in 1866, via their foreign sales agent "Colonel" Thomas Addis (a shadowy

The open breech of a Model 1895, with a British .303 cartridge about to be chambered. The extractor is visible on the top right of the sliding breech-block. (Laurie Landau/Bob Maze)

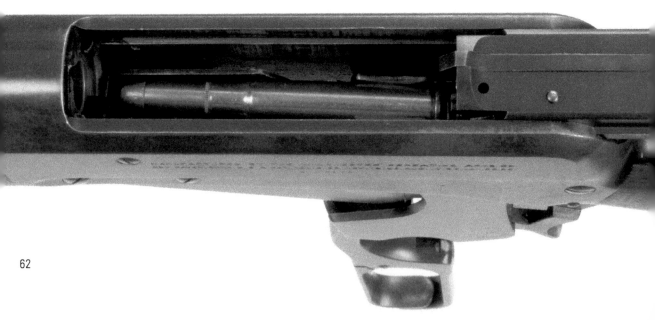

A French dispatch-rider of World War I, with a Model 1894 carbine slung over his back. (Michael F. Carrick)

character, his title apparently being self-appointed). His loyalty to Winchester was unwavering, though, for he acted as their foreign sales agent for 35 years. Benito Juárez, in opposition to the French-backed Emperor Maximilian I, had gained huge popular support, but he commanded an ill-equipped and poorly trained army, and his order for 1,000 rifles and a half-million rounds of ammunition was music to Oliver Winchester's ears, particularly as the contract was worth $57,000, or a little under a million dollars (£615,000) in today's values.

Other countries followed suit, with Chile and France placing modest orders in 1867, but it was an order from Turkey that was to galvanize Winchester's military sales. On November 9, 1870, a contract was signed for the supply of 5,000 carbines and 45,000 musket-pattern Model 1866s. Their use during the Russo-Turkish War of 1877–78 was to prove decisively that the era of the single-shot rifle had come to an end. The Russian soldiers were armed with either old Krnka muzzle-loaders converted to breech-loading or bolt-action Berdan single-shot rifles, while the Turks had the Peabody-Martini, virtually a duplicate of the single-shot British Martini-Henry. Turkish tactics were to engage the Russians at long range with the Peabodys and then, as they closed in, open an intense fire with their new Winchesters. They did this on repeated occasions, inflicting colossal casualties on the Russian forces. This culminated in the Siege of Plevna (July 1877), where the intense fire from the Ottoman lines proved insuperable. The Russian and Romanian assaults were launched in the teeth of the most devastating rapid fire from the Turkish defenders;

The Model 1895 in World War I (opposite)

By 1900 most European countries had re-equipped their armies with bolt-action magazine rifles. Russia too had adopted the M1891 Mosin-Nagant rifle, but shortages of weapons led the Russians to purchase around 300,000 Model 1895 Winchesters. Chambered for the 7.62×54mmR cartridge, the Winchesters were certainly powerful enough to be military weapons and when used in static positions, as shown here, their very rapid level of fire made them excellent defensive weapons. Austrian troops who attacked Russian soldiers armed with the Model 1895 suffered disproportionately high levels of casualties. But the Winchesters were not ideal for the conditions on the Eastern Front, where mud, dust, and snow were commonplace. The lever action left the magazine and receiver wide open to the ingress of debris, and in very cold weather the actions froze solid – proof, if it were needed, that the bolt-action rifle was superior for service use.

sending forward second and third waves served only to increase the slaughter. "Plevna is one of the few engagements which changed the course of history" (Taylor 1954: 245). Although the Turks were eventually overwhelmed by a Russian force five times their size, the conflict resulted in 20,000 Russian and Romanian dead, compared to 5,000 Ottoman. It appeared that at last, the wider world had sat up and begun to take notice of the new repeaters. But it was not to be, for although in 1878 and 1879 substantial numbers (the exact quantity is unknown) of Model 1873 muskets were sold to China, after this date military contracts virtually ceased for 35 years.

The outbreak of World War I, however, provided Winchester with a new outlet. Few people realize that in 1914 the French Government ordered 15,100 Model 1894 carbines with 20in barrels, and over 5 million rounds of Winchester .30-30 ammunition. Unusually, they were to be supplied by Remington Arms, which was already contracted to the French Government to provide rifles and ammunition. They were slightly modified with the addition of side-mounted sling swivels on the left front barrel-band and stock, the reason being they were all destined for the French Department of Military Transportation, which was responsible for horse-drawn transport and motorcycle couriers across the front. For a mounted man to carry a rifle comfortably, it needed to be slung flat across the back, hence the modified sling swivels. This was small beer, though, in comparison to the largest foreign military contract ever accepted by Winchester, which was signed on August 4, 1914.

This was a requirement to supply the Russian Army initially with 100,000 Model 1895 rifles, with a further 200,000 ordered in August

A Russian-contract Model 1895, showing the additional woodwork and bayonet lug, sling swivels, and ladder-pattern rear sight. (NRA Museums, NRAmuseums.com)

Russian soldiers in a defensive position with Model 1895s and fitted bayonets. (Stefan Brinski)

1915, along with 300 million cartridges. These long-barreled muskets were modified with the addition of wooden forends and bayonet lugs. All were chambered for the standard Russian 7.62×54mmR cartridge and they were unusual in also being provided with charger-guides so that the magazines could be topped up. The ammunition was actually a contentious issue with regard to these guns, for the Russians insisted on supplying their own cartridges for testing, despite the fact that Winchester were already tooled-up for mass production. This was to result in considerable conflict between the factory and Russian inspectors, as much of the Russian ammunition was of poor quality and rifles tested at the factory in the presence of the Russians often failed to perform properly, resulting in large numbers being rejected by them and being declared substandard. This posed a considerable problem for Winchester, who could not then include these rifles in the shipments, so many were returned to the factory and later sold into the domestic rifle market. There is also the strong possibility that, as there was nothing actually wrong with them, many were included in subsequent contracts supplied to other European countries such as Finland or Latvia.

Accounts of the use of any of these guns in combat are few, but during the Brusilov Offensive of June–September 1916 the Austro-Hungarian Army counterattacked the Russians. According to the Austrian official history of World War I:

> Our advancing soldiers were met with fierce fire from the entrenched Russians, who used their Maxim machine-guns to great effect, supported by repeating rifle-fire that proved insurmountable to overcome. We were forced to retreat with heavy losses and use our artillery, which was superior, to break up the enemy's lines.

After Russia reorganized its army in the 1930s, some 10,000 obsolete Model 1895s are believed to have been sent to the Spanish Republican Army for use during the Spanish Civil War (1936–39).

IMPACT
The Winchester's place in history

TECHNICAL IMPACT

Supplanting the single-shot rifle

The introduction of the first repeating rifles was without doubt a milestone in firearms development, for since the 18th century the single greatest desire on the part of designers and manufacturers had been to perfect a means by which a firearm could be repeatedly discharged. As is always the case, such desires were usually limited by the available technology of the period. It is not impossible that had Benjamin Tyler Henry invented his gun a decade earlier, it would have become nothing more than an interesting footnote in firearms history. Without an effective form of self-contained ammunition to use, the design would have failed. The coincidence of Henry's design with the perfection of metallic cartridges provided him with the wherewithal to produce a rifle that was a hitherto unimaginable leap forward in firearms technology. To modern eyes, accustomed as we are to the relentless march of modern science, it is impossible to realize exactly what that rifle represented when it first appeared.

In 1860, most of the long-arms in the world were muzzle-loading, single-shot weapons. The percussion cap had been in general use for about 30 years and the use of rifles for general service issue only for around 20 years. Combining these two technologies in the rifle-musket was considered at the time to be the greatest leap forward in arms technology since the invention of the flintlock. During the Civil War breech-loading was a novelty, and on the outbreak of war some units had even been armed with smoothbore muskets. Yet, out of the blue, one man appeared with a gun that was not only rifled but also breech-loading and fired a metallic cartridge. It could also genuinely fire one shot per second, which was almost unbelievable at a time when the best-trained soldiers could manage perhaps four shots a minute.

Little wonder, then, that many decried the new-fangled guns as impossible or unnecessary, wasteful, or just downright preposterous. So perhaps it was not entirely surprising that the Henrys were not at first a huge commercial success. The total sales of around 14,000 guns were reasonable but disappointing, yet this was as much due to public perception as the need for the mechanical system to be refined so that it was reliable. Of course, where new technology is concerned, virtually no mechanical system is perfect straight off the drawing board. It took the production of those 14,000 Henrys to show both Benjamin Tyler Henry and Oliver Winchester the direction in which they needed to travel. It also raised awareness among both the general public and the military about the limitations that their existing rifles imposed upon them. In the same way that the rifle-musket eventually supplanted the smoothbore, it was inevitable that, eventually, the same would happen with the repeater and the single-shot rifle.

On the battlefield

Just how important were the Winchesters in a military context? How great the Native American use of the Henry and Winchester rifles was in battle has been much disputed for many decades, but there is more proof emerging about the weapons used during the Indian Wars as a result of the considerable battlefield archaeology that has been undertaken over the past years. Although many locations have been closely examined, such as the Fetterman, Wagon Box, and Big Hole sites, probably the most contentious – but also the most investigated – has been the Little Bighorn battlefield in Montana. One problem in determining who fired what and at whom has been the fact that many of the scouts and civilians that accompanied Army units carried Henrys or Winchesters, as is evidenced by earlier accounts of their effectiveness in driving off Indian forays. In the instance of a large-scale battle such as Custer's ill-fated stand at the Little Bighorn, it is certain that the troopers involved carried only service carbines (.45-70 "Trapdoor" Springfields) and .45-caliber Colt single-action revolvers, and they had no lever-action weapons. Thus all the cartridge archaeology that has been unearthed can be very specifically categorized as either Army or Indian. What has emerged is that the Lakota, Cheyenne, and Arapaho warriors who took part were very well armed indeed. At least eight Model 1873 Winchesters were used, but this number is dwarfed by the estimated 62 Henry and Model 1866 rifles that have been identified from fired cases.

Charles H. Windolph, who survived the later Reno–Benteen fight at the Little Bighorn, said that he estimated from his direct experience a quarter of the total in terms of weapons carried by warriors were modern repeating rifles. This was a significant percentage when they were used against soldiers armed with what were generally regarded to be slower-firing, single-shot carbines. However, in 1879 the US Army conducted comparative tests to see just how effective the lever-action rifles were, and the results were rather surprising. The Henrys and Winchesters did not have the range of the cavalry Springfields – 200yd compared to 600yd. Neither did they have the Springfields' penetration of 11in of pine at 200yd, which was slightly more than double that achieved by a .44 bullet. However, it proved a surprise that the breech-loading carbines could be fired at the rate of 29 shots in two minutes, compared to the lever-actions' 33. This, theoretically, did not put the Army at that much of a disadvantage in an equal fight, but when used in close combat, against an enemy who did not show themselves except for a brief second at a time, then the Henrys and Winchesters must certainly have provided their owners with a firepower advantage.

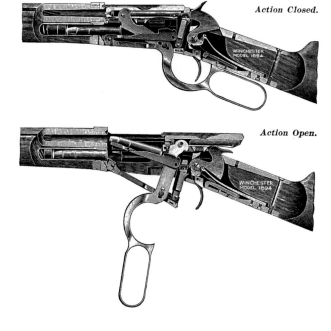

Action Closed.

Action Open.

One of Winchester's own sectional drawings of the action of the Model 1894. When compared to earlier models such as the 1866 or 1872, the relative complexity of the mechanism required to strengthen it is evident. (Author)

The triumph of the bolt-action rifle

While commercial sales began to pick up with the introduction of the later Winchesters, no one could have predicted that the military would actually move away from the lever-action, in favour of the slower, more reliable bolt-action. This was not the fault of Henry, Winchester, or even John Browning, for by its very nature the lever-action could not be easily adapted to being a military arm, which needed to be tough and soldier-proof. But the real problem lay with the Winchester's inability to handle

A rare picture of Russian troops on the Eastern Front during World War I, armed with Model 1895 Winchesters. The man at left has his bayonet fitted, while the soldier next to him has the lever lowered and is apparently loading his magazine. (Stefan Brinski)

A small but important breakthrough was Winchester's 1873 introduction of the first all-in-one reloading tool. This enabled a shooter to de-cap, re-charge and replace the bullet in an empty case with one pocket-sized tool. This example, for the .44-40 WCF (Winchester Center Fire) cartridge, is one of the earliest models. (Courtesy of Antique Arms, Inc.)

the powerful cartridges demanded by the military. The mechanism was just too fragile to withstand hard service use and abuse, despite the best efforts of Browning to strengthen it. The tubular magazine was outdated and unsafe with modern jacketed ammunition, and even the box magazine on the final incarnation, the Model 1895, was perilously open to dirt and mud. Its use by the Turkish and Russian armies, albeit in modest numbers, did at least prove that the rifles could provide an overwhelming superiority of fire, when correctly used.

Although in its later variants, the .30-caliber cartridge was quite effective, by the 1880s things had moved on and the concept of the lever-action rifle was simply not one that the world's armies were prepared to consider. But despite the failure of the guns to generate significant military orders, the Winchesters nevertheless fulfilled a valuable role, providing generations of settlers, trappers, homesteaders, and hunters with a solidly built, reliable rifle offering a rate of fire unmatched by any other weapons. In its larger calibers it eventually proved to be a competent hunting rifle, and in carbine form it was perfect for a mounted man, providing greater range and firepower than a revolver without being too heavy or cumbersome to handle.

COMMERCIAL IMPACT

Oddly, despite being the apogee of the lever-action design, the Model 1895 was to prove the most successful military rifle Winchester ever produced, for it was widely adopted by several armies in musket rifle form. But it also led to a final split between Browning and Winchester and the ending of the agreement that the company had with John Browning. In the early years this had doubtless served both parties well, but as the success of the marque continued, it seemed to Browning that the fees paid to him, which specifically excluded any royalties, were inadequate considering the burgeoning level of sales. Indeed, so profitable was the range of lever-actions that for 40 years from 1866 the Winchester Company would not have to borrow a single cent to fund its continuing research and manufacturing, an almost unequaled record in US manufacturing history.

Although Browning was never motivated by money, he certainly felt aggrieved that the existing arrangement was heavily weighted in Winchester's favor. Yet it seems ironic that the final split was to be the result not of money, or failure to improve the lever-actions' designs, but because of a shotgun. In 1887 Winchester had produced their lever-action shotgun, a cumbersome design that was quickly eclipsed by their iconic Model 1897 pump-action shotgun, one of the best-selling shotguns ever and one that became a legend in firearms history, with almost 1,250,000 being produced. But times were moving on; the public were becoming more interested in new types of guns, particularly semiautomatics, and Browning had been working on a revolutionary new self-loading shotgun.

Browning's new design was practical, reliable and potentially very lucrative but Bennett, with his inherent distrust of "new" technology, refused to proceed with it – and what Bennett said was law as far as Winchester was concerned. His attitude was not dissimilar to that of Brigadier General Ripley during the Civil War, who also believed that tried and tested technology was perfectly adequate and experimentation a waste of resources. Bennett knew and understood the lever-actions, but he disliked the new self-loaders. As Browning later wrote: "The factory was a temple and Bennett the high priest." Browning had considerable sympathy for him, though, writing:

> The automatic shotgun put him [Bennett] in a tough position. I'll bet he would had [*sic*] shelled out a hundred thousand dollars just to have it banished from the earth, leaving him with his levers and pumps [pump-action rifles and shotguns]. If he made the gun and it proved a failure, as he and his advisors seemed to have half suspected, it would leave a blot on the Winchester name. Even if he made it, and it proved a big success it would seriously hurt one of the best paying arms in his line, the '97 shotgun. If a competitor got it and it caught the popular fancy, he'd be left a long jump behind in an important branch of the business. That's why he marked time for two years, and why, once I forced a showdown, I got so mad. (Quoted in Browning & Gentry 1987: 45)

Bennett's reluctance to take on the new gun and Browning's refusal simply to hand over the patent rights with no royalty agreement caused an impasse that led to a final break between the two and the ending of a partnership in 1902 that had endured successfully for 20 years. Others were not slow to take up the new design. Browning went to Fabrique Nationale d'Armes de Guerre in Liége, Belgium, a company that positively jumped at the chance to manufacture the new design. Remington Arms took on the manufacturing rights in the USA and began producing their hugely popular semiautomatic shotgun range in 1905; within a few years, semiautomatic rifles and shotguns had created a whole new marketplace in the firearms industry. It was by no means the end of the manufacturing of the lever-actions, but it lost Winchester the edge the company needed to keep ahead of its competitors and it subsequently took ten years of experimentation for the firm to come up with its own design.

In spite of the financial success of the August 1914 Russian contract, which netted Winchester $10.95 million ($190 million/£121.3 million today), such sporadic military sales were insufficient to warrant the continual production of the Model 1895 rifles, which had generally sold

The action of the Model 1894 open, with a .30-caliber Winchester cartridge about to be chambered. To date over 5.5 million have been sold. (Laurie Landau/Bob Maze)

OPPOSITE A Winchester flyer showing the available Model 1892 rifles. From the top these are the Sporting model, De-luxe half-stocked model, the extremely popular saddle-ring carbine, the unusual short-magazine carbine and the military musket. The cutaways illustrate how the toggle mechanism had to be strengthened to cope with the more powerful cartridges. (Author)

poorly to the civilian market, and in 1940 production belatedly ceased. This did not, of course, signal the end of the marque as other models, such as the Model 1892 and Model 1894, continued to sell well, but it was perhaps an indication that times and tastes were changing; before long, that change would mean the death-knell for Winchester.

Despite the company's reputation for manufacturing lever-action rifles, one of its greatest financial successes was the tiny Model 1903 .22-caliber self-loading rifle, the design of which has remained unchanged to this day. By the late 1920s Winchester had diversified into different areas of sporting goods, hardware, tools, even batteries, but it had conspicuously failed to maintain its brand leadership in respect of its firearms. Other makers such as Marlin, Savage, and FN Browning were proving tough competition and the demand for the old lever-action rifles had tailed off. In 1931 Winchester Repeating Arms went into receivership and was bought by Olin Industries in 1944. Through two world wars, the company continued to make small arms at its New Haven plant, but its fortunes began to wane in the wake of the glut of firearms that appeared post-1945. Additionally, the design of Winchester's guns was simply too labor-intensive to be competitive, and by the 1960s the company was in dire straits. In the wake of spiraling labor costs through the 1970s, allied to a bitter strike in 1979–80, it was believed firearms could no longer be profitably manufactured. A poorly judged attempt to manufacture cheaper rifles was largely shunned by the public. In 1980 the company was sold to its employees, becoming the US Repeating Arms Company; sadly, this merely proved a stopgap measure and it went bankrupt in 1989, the assets being sold to FN Herstal. The New Haven factory closed in January 2006, although Olin continued to manufacture Winchester-brand ammunition.

However, new generations of shooters imbued with the history associated with Winchester rifles began to create a demand for a product that was no longer available. In 2008 Fabrique Nationale d'Herstal of Belgium, who had purchased the Winchester name, resumed manufacture of some iconic Winchester lever-action models such as the 1885, 1886, and 1892, and in a landmark decision, resumed production of the hugely popular Model 1894 lever-action as well as other modern designs. Other

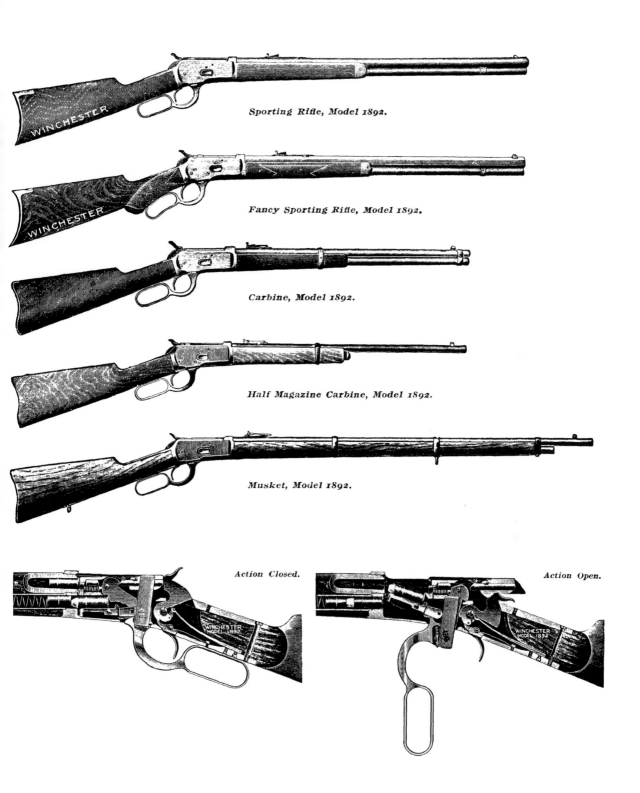

Sporting Rifle, Model 1892.

Fancy Sporting Rifle, Model 1892.

Carbine, Model 1892.

Half Magazine Carbine, Model 1892.

Musket, Model 1892.

Action Closed.

Action Open.

models are being manufactured under license in Japan. In a final, fitting tribute, exact replicas of the original Henry rifle can now once again be bought from the Henry Rifle Company of New Jersey – and they are made in America.

CULTURAL IMPACT

It is usually very difficult to decide exactly what effect the introduction of a single type of small arm has had on society in general. Usually, the answer would be "minimal." Sometimes the type of gun itself proves to be such a radical step forward in mechanical development that it acquires for itself a place in the technical hall of fame, without necessarily achieving huge sales or fame in combat. The Gatling gun could well be cited as an example of this, being the first truly workable rapid-fire gun. In other instances, success can simply be measured in sheer sales volume; there is little doubt that in terms of technology the AK-47 would not even make it into the top ten, for its basis was that of tried and tested designs that pre-dated World War II; the AK itself is not revolutionary. But its production success has been nothing short of phenomenal, with world-wide manufacture of the AK and its variants approaching the 100 million mark, and it is the most prominent firearm seen in television news footage today. Sometimes fame rests upon the visual rather than the commercial, for some firearms have achieved an iconic status without being either particularly efficient, or unusually technically advanced. The Luger semiautomatic is possibly the most immediate example of the former, for while it borrowed the beautifully made and complex mechanism from the earlier Borchardt pistol, it was neither very accurate to shoot nor reliable in the field, but almost anyone with even the sketchiest knowledge of guns will recognize one. As an example of the latter, the Colt single-action must rate among the top contenders.

Then there is a category of guns that transcends all of the reasons outlined above. They were the first examples of their genre, they changed the perception of what a firearm could do, they sold in their hundreds of thousands and still continue to be made to this day, and they spawned imitators, creating a huge collector network. Moreover, they became the industry standard for film and television, resulting in exposure (some might say over-exposure) to the public at large on a scale far beyond that of any other firearm. The two guns that immediately spring to mind are the Winchester rifle, and Colt single-action revolver, but of the two, it is only the Winchester that fulfills all of the criteria that make it unique. The Colt, for all its popularity, was merely an advanced variant of existing revolvers and it utilized no really advanced technology. On the other hand the Winchester – or more specifically the Henry rifle – transformed the long-arm from a cumbersome, slow-firing weapon to a rapid-fire, take-anywhere arm that was as practical on a wagon-train as it was in the hands of a hunter or soldier. Not only could it be fired from horseback, it could be loaded as well, something that could not be easily done with most other rifles.

Considering how relatively short the era of the American West was (generally cited as starting with the Louisiana Purchase of 1803 and lasting to about 1900), its legacy has remained undimmed to the present day. To a great extent this has been due to the powerful imagery used to depict that time. But it was particularly the medium of cinema that was to enhance and perpetuate the myth of the Old West, and it did so by prominently featuring the one tool that above all others made the conquest of the West possible – the firearm. Guns became a focal point of many of these films, and their constant exposure led to generations of film-goers, who had little or no physical contact with guns, being able instantly to identify the firearms being used. Indeed, one of the very first cinema films ever made was a 'western' called *The Great Train Robbery*, in 1903. Of all of these guns, two makes stand head and shoulders above the rest: the Colt revolver and the Winchester rifle. In fact, so frequently were they the only firearms used in films that many people could be forgiven for thinking that they were the only guns ever carried westwards. While this is patently untrue, it does emphasize just how powerful the big screen has been in shaping a view of history that is not accurate. Most of the main Winchester models have featured at some time on the big screen, but as film-makers have become more accurate in their portrayal of the myriad guns that were used in the West, so there has been a greater exposure of some of the models that have hitherto been overlooked.

Probably the best example is the Henry rifle, which for all its historical importance, was never used in a film until 1962, when one was carried by Henry Fonda in *How the West Was Won*. In fairness, it might be argued that the Henry, for all its ground-breaking technology, was not actually a very good rifle. Nevertheless, it was by any standards a quantum leap forward in firearms design, although that crucial fact is probably lost on film-makers. It is perhaps worth noting that shortly afterward its first appearance, a "Henry" rifle was supposedly carried in the Clint Eastwood "spaghetti western" *The Good, The Bad and The Ugly* (1966), but due to their rarity and value an altered Model 1866 was used. Eastwood is known for his interest in and knowledge of firearms and it was supposedly at his request that this contemporary and unusual rifle was represented. In four subsequent decades it appeared just eleven times in various films, but with the introduction of the new genre of "realistic" Westerns that number has been greatly exceeded since the year 2000. If the Henry was not regarded

There were many black cowboys working the ranches in the West, and they earned a reputation for toughness and reliability. This is the picturesquely named Nat Love photographed in a studio with the tools of his trade: a saddle, rope, gun-belt, and Winchester Model 1894. (Denver Public Library)

as mainstream for the film-going public, then the same cannot be said of the later Winchester models.

The first Winchester to really become a screen icon was the Model 1866 Yellow Boy carried by John Wayne in the 1948 film *Fort Apache*. The fact that the US Army were never issued with Winchesters did not concern directors of the time. The rifles looked good, with their distinctive yellow receivers and rapid fire, which translated well on the big screen. Interestingly almost all the Native Indians were equipped with Winchester by the studios and the visual appeal of the Winchesters ensured that they were a prominent part of the Western movie arsenal from around this date. One could go so far as to say that the visual myth began at this time that no one who ventured west of the Platte River carried any guns except Colts or Winchesters.

If the Model 1866 had gained some small fame on screen, it was nothing compared to the impact that the Model 1873 was to have. If the Winchester had not quite achieved icon status by then, it did after the film *Winchester '73* starring James Stewart came out in 1950. The film was unusual for several reasons, for it was the first time in movie history that a film was made specifically about a firearm. It also wove a certain amount of truth into the plot, portraying the Indians who fought at Custer's ill-fated battle at the Little Bighorn as predominantly carrying Winchesters, which was at least partly true. But it also advertised the little-appreciated fact that Winchester had produced a range of expensive and rare limited editions, marketed as the "One of a Hundred" and "One of a Thousand" rifles. Indeed, so keen was the director of the film, Anthony Mann, for authenticity where the rifles were concerned, that an appeal was launched through the gun press and by means of 150,000 posters appealing for information on the whereabouts and numbers of genuine surviving "One of a Thousand" Model 1873s. As a result they found 23 and used one for the film, with James Stewart reportedly being presented with the rifle after the end of filming. The Model 1873 rifle arguably became more famous than many actors of the period, making 44 appearances in subsequent films.

Without a doubt, though, the single most influential figure to use the Winchester was John Wayne, who had a personal liking for the models and carried them in no fewer than 40 films. In 11 of those films he carried a Model 1892 saddle-ring carbine with a modified large-ring 'Mare's leg' lever, most memorably for his performance in *True Grit* (1969) which finally won him both a Golden Globe and an Oscar. On the small screen the Model 1892 also became the star of a hugely successful television production, *The Rifleman*, starring Chuck Connors, who also carried a large-ring Model 1892 throughout the series, which ran from 1958 to 1963. The author recalls watching the programs as a small boy and vowing to own a Winchester '92 one day, which sadly he never has. This was not the case for Connors, who was personally presented with two of the Winchesters. It could even be argued that in terms of film appearances, for sheer numbers the Model 1892 deserved its own Oscar, as to date it has been used in no fewer than 73 films and a dozen TV series. Sometimes the visual need clearly overcomes the

OPPOSITE A Welsh immigrant, David Hughes, who worked in Arizona towards the end of the Western era. He is pictured here (*c*.1896) in his work clothes. Wrinkled trousers, stained shirt, frayed leggings, and dust-covered boots are evidence of a man who has just climbed off his horse. His rifle is the Model 1894 carbine; the revolver appears to be an unusual Colt Bisley model. (Arizona Historical Society)

historical where film studios are concerned. In the 1941 film, *They Died with Their Boots On*, the Indians fighting at the Little Bighorn in 1876 were portrayed carrying Winchester Model 1892 rifles!

Although almost indistinguishable from the Model '92, the Model 1894 must come a close second in terms of screen-time. For some reason it never quite seems to have held the visual appeal of its predecessor, but has still managed 40 films, and one features frequently in the TV series *Longmire*. Most of its use has been post-1960, possibly because of its similarity with earlier types and the ease with which the model can still be bought. This makes it more attractive and cost-effective to use, particularly in more modern times, when prices for original rifles have become very high. There is also the requirement for these guns to fire blanks and the more modern calibers' chambering make it easier for film armorers to secure the sometimes large quantities of ammunition needed. The last of the lever-actions, the Model 1895, is still rather under-represented on the big screen, having a mere 18 appearances to its credit, the majority of them relatively recent. It is perhaps an indication of how producers have been looking more closely at historical accuracy than in the past. In the 1969 film *Butch Cassidy and the Sundance Kid* the Bolivian Army are shown using Model 1895s; there is evidence that Mexico actually sold several hundred to Bolivia.

The surge of interest in Western firearms has meant that there are many good reproductions available, and most of those seen on screen will be modern Italian- or US-made copies; these are cheap and in many instances, arguably better made than the originals. This has greatly enlarged the potential arsenal from which film and TV companies can pick for added historical accuracy. There are, for example, more Henrys available today than there were when they were in production.

CONCLUSION

Many claims have been made about the popularity of various firearms over the years, but such is the iconic status of the Winchester, that it is probably not far from the truth that it and its cousin the Colt Single Action are known as "the guns that won the West." After over a century both are still in production in virtually unchanged form, a testimony to the excellence of their original design, and they still feature frequently on both the large and small screens. Despite this fame, it is a fact that neither the Winchester nor the Colt was the first in its field; repeating rifles such as the Spencer had been adopted into military service in 1860 and workable revolvers had been in existence since the 1820s. Even so, while Colt retained the tried and tested mechanical system of the revolvers, the Winchesters were in a league of their own, for there was nothing like them. Indeed, there is still nothing else (with the possible exception of loading a pump-action shotgun) that has the same feel, sound or cachet as dropping the loading lever and chambering a cartridge on a Winchester.

At a time when even breech-loading was considered a new and exciting development and magazine rifles were rare, to combine both breech-loading with a magazine and then add in a repeating action raised the game to another level. Even if not that many buyers were initially ready to exchange their reliable old rifle-muskets for the new-fangled guns, it showed what could be done, and in doing so Winchester forced other manufacturers – who were prepared to continue producing what they had always produced – to re-evaluate their position. Between them, Benjamin Tyler Henry and Oliver Winchester effectively changed the rules where firearms design was concerned. The fact that the guns are still in production today speaks volumes for their popularity and practicality. Gun buyers do not part with their money easily and they demand a product that is reliable, accurate, and tough. The Winchesters have now been proving that they meet those exacting demands for over 150 years. The Winchester was and still is, to many people, the gun that won the West.

Barnes, F.C. (2012). *Cartridges of the World.* 13th edition. Iola, WI: Gun Digest.

Bell, W.A. (1869). *New Tracks in North America.* London: Chapman & Hall.

Browning, J.M. & C. Gentry (1987). *John Browning, American Gunmaker.* Ogden, UT: The Browning Company.

Cleveland, H.W.S. (1864). *Hints to Riflemen.* New York, NY: D. Appleton & Co.

Davis, Britton (1976). *The Truth about Geronimo.* Lincoln, NE: Bison Books. Originally published 1929.

Dodge, Colonel R.I. (1883). *Our Wild Indians.* Hartford, CT: A.D. Worthington & Co.

Edwards, W.B. (1982). *Civil War Guns.* Edison, NJ: Castle Books.

Garavaglia, L.A. & C.G. Worman (1984). *Firearms of the American West, Vol. 1: 1803–1865.* Albuquerque, NM: University of New Mexico Press.

Garavaglia, L.A. & C.G. Worman (1985). *Firearms of the American West, Vol. 2: 1866–1894.* Albuquerque, NM: University of New Mexico Press.

Garcia, Andrew (1967). *A Tough Trip Through Paradise, 1878–79.* Moscow, ID: University of Idaho Press.

Jinks, R.G. (1977). *History of Smith and Wesson.* Los Angeles, CA: Beinfeld Publications.

Kirkland, K.D. (1990). *America's Premier Gunmakers.* London: Bison Books.

Langford, D.P. (1893). *Vigilante Days and Ways.* New York, NY: D.D. Merrill Co.

McAulay, J.D. (1987). *Civil War Breech Loading Rifles.* Woonsocket, RI: Mowbray Publishing.

McDowel, R.B. (1985). *Evolution of the Winchester.* Tacoma, WA: Armory Publications.

Murphy, J.M. (1880). *Sporting Adventures in the Far West.* New York, NY: Harper & Brothers.

Ordway, E. (1925) "Reminiscences," in *Annals of Wyoming*, Vol. 5, No. 4, June 1925: 149–57.

Parsons, J.E. (1966). *The First Winchester.* New York, NY: Winchester Press.

Pegler, Martin (1998). *Firearms of the American West.* Ramsbury: Crowood.

Roosevelt, T.H. (1885). *Hunting Trips of a Ranchman: Hunting Trips on the Prairie and in the Mountains.* New York, NY: G.P. Putnam's Sons.

Roosevelt, T.H. (1905). *Outdoor Pastimes of an American Hunter.* New York, NY: Scribner & Sons.

Roosevelt, T.H. (1910). *African Game Trails.* Two volumes. New York, NY: Scribner & Sons.

Schultz, J.W. (1962). *Blackfeet and Buffalo: Memories of Life Among the Indians.* Norman, OK: University of Oklahoma Press.

Taylor, A.J.P. (1954). *The Struggle for Mastery in Europe 1848–1918.* Oxford: Clarendon Press.

Taylor, R.F. (1932). "Rifles and Pistols of the Southwest," in *American Rifleman*, Vol. LXXX, No. 5, May 1932: 37.

Wells, Philip (1948). "Ninety-six Years among the Indians of the Northwest," in *North Dakota History*, Vol. XV, Nos 2–4, January–October 1948: 26.

Williamson, H.F. (1952). *Winchester, the Gun that Won the West.* New York, NY: Barnes & Co.

Wilson, N.C. (1987). *Treasure Express: Epic Days of the Wells Fargo.* Glorieta, NM: Rio Grande.

Wilson, R.L. (1991). *Winchester: An American Legend.* New York, NY: Random House.

INDEX